10/17/14

The Courage to Remember

Dear Beverly
I hope you find
this story interesting

The Courage to Remember

PTSD — From Trauma To Triumph

Lester Tenney

Lester Tenney Publishing
Carlsbad, CA

The information in this volume is not intended as a substitute for consultation with
healthcare professionals. In addition, the author and publisher assume no liability of
any kind whatsoever resulting from the use of or reliance upon the contents of this
book.

Photo credit page 39: Life Magazine, 1943

Hardcover ISBN 978-0-9906380-0-1
Paperback ISBN 978-0-9906380-1-8

Lester Tenney Publishing
Carlsbad, CA

Printed in the United States of America
PubLitho, Draper, UT

10 9 8 7 6 5 4 3 2 1

This book is dedicated to my family,

who has suffered immeasurably

because of my PTSD.

Acknowledgments

A special thanks goes my editor, Jane Ploetz, for her continual devotion to this project. Her work was a labor of love, and I appreciated her thoughtful input and meaningful suggestions.

Thanks also to my fellow residents at La Costa Glen who took the time to read and evaluate my story. Many thanks to Mary Ann Yuhas, Nic and Sharon Wood, who reviewed the manuscript and encouraged me to publish. Shirley Collins and Gene Ragan undertook the painstaking responsibility of proofreading the final text, and did a remarkably thorough job. For his original cover design, deepest appreciation to Doug Strole.

Thanks to my literary agent, Bob Diforio, for consistent support and encouragement.

No book of this magnitude can be brought to print without the know-how of members of the publication team. I was very fortunate to have the outstanding graphic designer, Rachael Gibson, and a dynamic book production guru, Mr. Bruce Bracken. I thank them for their dedication to this project.

Most of all, I am indebted to my family: to Betty's two sons Don and Ed and to my son Glenn, who urged me to finish it. My deepest gratitude goes to Betty, my wife of fifty-five years, who brought me happiness I never thought possible, and taught me that when values are clear, decisions are easy.

Table of Contents

Foreword

by Alisa D. Gean, MD

As a physician who has studied brain injury for over three decades, I am honored to provide a medical review of Lester Tenney's story and struggle with Post-Traumatic Stress Disorder. This topic is dear to my heart. In addition to my primary role as an academic civilian physician, I spent two brief tours during 2007 and 2008 at Landstuhl Regional Medical Center, the largest military base outside of the United States where all wounded warriors are treated immediately after being injured in Iraq and Afghanistan. I have witnessed firsthand the sacrifice, suffering and courage of our nation's military. As such, I am extremely grateful to Dr. Tenney for speaking up about PTSD in the context of his personal journey. *The Courage to Remember* describes his captivating experience with poignant clarity, but perhaps more importantly, it provides insight and wise advice to people suffering from PTSD.

Personally, I prefer to use the acronym PTS, as the diagnosis is not really a disorder – it is a very normal reaction to a very abnormal situation. The Canadian military uses the term "operational stress injury." In my opinion, it is an injury, a virtual laceration of the human psyche, not a flaw or weakness in the individual. Having trouble processing trauma is a very human, understandable reaction as described by Dr. Tenney in *The Courage to Remember*. Indeed, people who have no difficulty seeing horrible things and touching body parts of people they knew and considered friends, may be the ones with a disorder.

What is PTS? Medically, PTS is defined as an anxiety disorder characterized by three symptoms: avoidance, re-experiencing, and hyper arousal (or hyper vigilance).

Les points out that unfortunately, as is often the case with human trauma: the full extent of psychological injury is often hidden from plain view (i.e., the so-called 'walking wounded'). But the symptoms are there just the same. Some individuals cannot stop the hyper vigilance that worked so well in combat, once they come home.

Other symptoms Les pointed out may include emotional instability, impulsivity, irritability, sleep disorders, difficulty concentrating, slowed thinking, and short-term memory problems, terror and intrusive nightmares. Depression, as explained, is particularly common, disrupting both the life of the individual and their social network.

It's important to remember that PTS can appear long after the traumatic event. It may follow a relatively asymptomatic latency period that can sometimes last for years.

It is believed that 20% of all troops returning from Iraq and Afghanistan may be suffering from PTS. These victims are added to the 500,000 existing Vietnam veterans with chronic PTS who incur estimated disability costs of $4.3 billion per year. The financial cost of PTS and depression among service members is estimated to exceed $6 billion in the first two years following deployment alone. The percentage of the nation's daily suicides committed by veterans was 21% in 2010 (22 per day).

This epidemic of military suicides does not include civilian suicides stemming from PTS. The "battlefield of the mind" is not limited to individuals deployed to a front-line combat zone or victims of terrorism. Exposure to civilian trauma such as rape, natural disasters, child and domestic abuse, and even car accidents has been linked to the development of PTSD. Post -Traumatic Stress affects much more than the mind. In addition to the emotional wreckage, the physiological effects of PTS can take a tremendous toll one's body. PTS is an even bigger beast than the staggering statistics mentioned above suggest. PTS substantially increases the risk for age-related diseases, such as cardiovascular, autoimmune, and neurodegenerative diseases, along with early mortality. Changes in sleep patterns among patients following traumatic experiences can contribute to disease persistence. Depression, a common symptom of PTS, triggers stress hormones that induce inflammation and plaque buildup in arteries, which may accelerate heart disease. It is also associated with unemployment, divorce, substance abuse, domestic violence, and homelessness.

PTS Treatment.   How, then, does one overcome life-altering adversity and succeed in life?   I found the answers to most of issues in Tenney's *The Courage to Remember*. Those who are suffering must get help, but access to adequate numbers of qualified medical professionals is a challenge. It takes time and effort, it's complicated, but it works. Like other injuries, PTS is treatable. As Tenney explained, Cognitive-Behavioral Therapy (CBT), psychoanalysis, body-oriented therapy, educational strategies are all potentially helpful. PTS has a wide range of symptoms, courses, and "cures" based on multiple factors.

However, a one-size-fits-all approach is insufficient, and multi-modality treatment will likely be necessary.

In addition, despite the growing problem, a serious obstacle remains to fixing it; there must be a cultural change with destigmatization of the injury. There is a common fear in those who seek help for mental problems. Professional athletes, soldiers, and even civilians fear they will be perceived as weak and that acknowledging a need for help will damage their career and in certain jobs, lose their security clearance. Indeed, over half of all soldiers surveyed in one study said that leadership would treat them differently if they sought counseling. My hope is that referring to the condition as an injury rather than a disorder would encourage more troops to seek treatment. Commanding Officers, fellow soldiers, and loved ones need to be trained to recognize symptoms, signs and behavior of PTS and speak up about it. People receiving treatment for PTS are not damaged goods.

The Courage to Remember addresses all of these issues. A timely and powerful reminder of the prevalence of PTS in society today, it provides valuable psychological tools to help patients, as well as their family and friends, deal with emotional recovery.

Tenney gives numerous additional helpful hints for dealing, and healing, from PTS relevant to all who suffer in receiving support, grounding, and reducing their anxiety. Some of these include: 1) the power of forgiveness (not necessarily condoning or forgetting), 2) the role of sharing one's struggles with a network of supporting friends and family (breaking through this resistance to seek help is among the greatest challenges), 3) taking "small rather than big steps" to recovery, 4) adopting an "attitude of gratitude", 5) "helping others will help yourself," and many others. He stresses that one cannot defend oneself alone from PTS, but victory is possible. It is strong, so you must be stronger.

Americans must know that the scars from PTS are very real and in many ways, more painful than the ones caused by bullets or shrapnel. No one should underestimate the power of PTS — it has no soul and fights only for yours. Dr. Tenney's fight to return to health isn't over, but it's manageable, because it is defined by a clear set of with specific methods of treatment that produce visible results. Les has helped make this invisible injury more visible by speaking up about this global "silent epidemic." He is an extremely credible voice for others who currently cannot, or are unwilling to speak. We should never forget that PTS deals with the most complex organ in the body, in very complex individuals, who are injured in very complex ways.

So, thank you, Les, for sharing the lessons you've learned over the last seventy years. As you have often quoted, "Life is 10% what happens to you and 90% what you make of it." Thank you for sharing both your 10% and your 90%. The scars in your mind, like those of your body, motivated you to tell your story, and in doing so, you will help others who are suffering through PTS darkness and pain. Like you, they will not only survive... they will thrive.

Alisa D. Gean, MD, Professor of Neuroradiology,
Neurology, and Neurological Surgery
University of California, San Francisco
Brain and Spinal center (BASIC)
San Francisco General Hospital

Foreword

by Congressman Darrell Issa

Lester (Les) Tenney is an American icon, ninety-four years old and still going strong. He doesn't believe in quitting, he only believes in marching forward, taking one step after the other, until he reaches his goal. He believes you get in life what you want by going after it. Dr. Tenney explained to me that he was writing this book because he believed he could help others who suffer the same stress-related problems that he's grappled with for seven decades. He then said, "If I can accomplish that in my last years of life I will feel that I've truly accomplished a purpose for living."

When Lester asked me to write the Foreword for this book, I gratefully accepted with the understanding that being part of such an endeavor carries a responsibility to the men and women who have experienced terrible horrors and are in the midst of recovering from their ordeals.

As the Member of Congress who has represented the Marines and Sailors at Camp Pendleton, California for the last fourteen years, I have witnessed firsthand the sacrifice, suffering and courage of our nation's troops during a time of war. Their stories and accomplishments are nothing less than inspirational.

The Courage to Remember lays out a timely and powerful message for our active and returning service members. Les Tenney's words are filled with wisdom and his book contains a powerful message of healing for those who are suffering from Post-Traumatic Stress Disorder (PTSD).

After more than a decade at war, more than 460,000 of our military members who served in Iraq and Afghanistan have been diagnosed with PTSD. This terrible injury can cripple lives, destroy relationships, and has frequently led to individuals taking their own life.

Dr. Tenney's advice and lessons, learned through his own terrible treatment during World War II, offer an empathic and personal reflection on how to begin the healing process and reclaim control of one's life.

Les Tenney is one of only about ten surviving members to have experienced the gruesome Bataan Death March while serving in the Army in the Philippines. After more than 120 days of brutal hand-to-hand combat with the Japanese, thousands of Americans and Filipinos were marched more than eighty miles, in temperatures that reached more than one-hundred degree, to their first prison camp, Camp O'Donnell. In unflinching detail, Dr. Tenney recounts the violence and torture that he witnessed and endured, including decapitations, individuals being pierced by bayonets and people buried alive. The march killed thousands of people and remains one of the worst war crimes committed by a nation during World War II.

Les Tenney survived forty-two months of brutal and dehumanizing captivity at the hands of the imperial Japanese government. Even after the war ended and he returned back to the United States, Lester came to realize that while he was physically free from his captors, there were other wounds that were not so easily healed.

With poignant clarity Dr. Tenney describes how hard it is for someone to connect with others who have not gone through the same or similar experience, and the loneliness and personal disconnect from society that follows. To cope with the "moral injury" of combat Dr. Tenney brings readers along on his own personal journey where he eventually finds a path to healing.

The Courage to Remember offers valuable tools and those who have been through the worst atrocities to never forget what happened, but to learn that forgiveness heals both parties. As Dr. Tenney writes, "By giving back you restore balance in the world. As much as you have suffered, you have the capacity to turn that suffering into goodness."

This book sets out a template to encourage those suffering with PTSD to take proactive steps in their recovery and help them lead the lives that they want and deserve.

Dr. Tenney writes with the skill of an orator: simple, factual, and thorough. His personal experiences mirror the experiences of the men and women he wrote this book for. One of the most heart-warming things I've ever been witness to is Les Tenney's willingness and ability to forgive his enemies for the barbaric treatment perpetrated on him during his captivity. As much as his service and the horrors he endured, his ability to forgive makes him a true hero.

Like I have, I believe you will also become so captivated with this book you will not be able to put it down. *The Courage to Remember* is a great companion for those suffering from the stresses of war. I highly recommend this book.

Preface

Why would I, a comfortably retired man of ninety-four, want to undertake the enormous task of writing a book at this stage of my life? What can I offer you of value from my experiences?

You deserve an answer to these questions, and yet, it's hard to know where to start. The truth is, it took me more than fifty years before I could even begin to talk about my past. It was too painful.

I am one of the few remaining survivors of the Bataan Death March in the Philippines in World War II, who became a Prisoner of War enslaved by the Japanese for three-and-a-half years. I survived four years of events so barbaric, inhumane, and brutal that most people could never imagine them. In fact, I thought my story of extreme trauma was the rare exception.

Yet, when invited to talk about how I survived these experiences, I'll often ask, by a show of hands, "How many of you have survived a traumatic event in your life?" I explain that "traumatic stress" is caused by more than breaking a leg, or getting stuck between floors on an elevator. It's from things like physical assault from abuse or rape, the unexpected death of a loved one, the combat of war, becoming a prisoner of war, or suddenly being homeless from a hurricane, flood or tornado. It can also be caused by helplessly witnessing another's death, or the trauma of having your life placed on hold while you await a heart valve replacement.

Each time I ask how many others have had even one of these experiences, I am continually amazed by the number of hands. The fact is, in a roomful of around 150 people, a hundred or so will raise their hands every time. Research confirms this. Two out of every three people will experience a serious trauma before their lives are out.

To me, that means that life is very hard for most of us. Chances are very good that someone you know, someone you love, or even you yourself, have survived some very difficult times.

Most folks who survive these events are able to go on with their lives. People always say, "Time heals all wounds," and for most of us, it does. You just have to give time enough time.

But for some of us, time stops ticking. Our lives go on "hold," sometimes for years. We get stuck in the past, reliving horrible scenes over and over. Or we avoid situations or people that trigger painful flashbacks. Or we are overly anxious about an unknown future. In my war, they called it "Battle Fatigue" or "Shell Shock." Only after the 1980s was it first seriously studied and given a different name: Post-Traumatic Stress Disorder, or PTSD. The symptoms, however, have always been the same.

Because of my past experiences, I'm familiar with many of those symptoms. For years, I felt the loneliness and isolation in a roomful of family or friends who seemed like strangers to me. I felt like I couldn't tell anyone about what I had experienced because they could never understand. I suffered the sleepless nights, the terrifying nightmares. I was filled with anger. But hardest of all to bear was the tremendous sense of guilt I suffered, always foremost in my mind: the guilt of surviving when so many of my friends died. I would think of them lying dead on the side of the road leading out of Bataan, or at the bottom of the ocean. I was haunted by this guilt for fifty years. All those years I asked myself, "Why, God, why did I survive when so many of my buddies did not?" For years, I had no answer.

Now, after all those years of questioning, I think I finally have the answer. I am writing now, after another twenty years, to share with you how I finally achieved peace of mind. It is to tell my story of how I was able to learn to live a different life, a life at whose core is friendship, love, God and forgiveness. It was not easy. It took many years, and was one of the most difficult battles of my life. In many ways, I felt that dying would have been easier; it's the living that's hard. Along the way I discovered that I had strengths within me I didn't even realize were there.

I'm not a professional health-care provider or a clinical psychologist. I'm just one man who has walked the path. And now, after all these years, I'm a little deaf, a little blind, three inches shorter and ten pounds heavier, I limp when I walk and I hiss when I speak. My hearing and my teeth were destroyed in Japan; I wear a hearing aid and have dentures supplied by the Veterans Administration, and a cow's valve in my chest. But nothing, absolutely nothing, can destroy my hope and my spirit.

Maybe you will see yourself in these pages, or find some answers to your hard questions. That is why I've found the courage to open my life up to you. If I can help someone else get their life back, too, then it all will have been worthwhile.

Some will live…

"Living has taught me that war does not determine who is right; it only determines who is left."

Chapter One
The Fight To Survive

My story begins over seventy years ago.

Most Americans know December 7, 1941 as the date the Japanese bombed Pearl Harbor. What many do not know is that the Japanese did not only attack Pearl Harbor, but also bombed seven additional strategic strongholds in the Pacific and Asia. One of these was Clark Airfield in the Philippines where I was stationed with Company B of the 192nd Tank Battalion. At 12:25 p.m., I watched in horror as bodies, buildings and tents flew through the air. For ninety minutes that seemed like days, their Zero aircraft bombed and strafed anything left that moved. Within minutes, all our US Army airplanes, B-16s, B-17s, and P-40s, parked on the tarmac like a bunch of sitting ducks, were destroyed. Since our Navy had already moved their ships away from Manila to other ports, by that afternoon we were completely defenseless. And that was only the beginning.

Within two months of the start of the war, our troops on Bataan were placed on half-rations, and lacked even the most basic necessities for combat. To make matters worse, on March 11th General MacArthur not only abandoned us for Australia, but also ordered moving all our remaining food, medical supplies, and ammunition to Corregidor, the island fortress of the Philippines known as "The Rock." By the time the Japanese combat forces came in for the kill, we were down to eating iguanas, horses, monkeys and snakes. Our medical supplies were so low, the nurses had to boil used bandages to sterilize them for re-use on the wounded. We fought valiantly, night and day, sometimes hand-to-hand, for 123 days, three times longer than the Japanese ever anticipated. But after running out of most essentials, those of us who managed to survive were either severely wounded, or suffering from diseases like malaria, beriberi, or dysentery. Pushed back by the Japanese almost to the water's edge, the situation looked bleak.

As the Japanese forces approached ours on Bataan, it became obvious to our commanding officer, General Edward King, that surrender was the only way he could save any of his troops. King said, "If I do not surrender today, Bataan will go down in the history books as the worst slaughter of the 20th century. "

And so, on April 9, 1942, the warriors on Bataan surrendered. It was the same date in 1865 of another infamous surrender, that of General Lee to General Grant. Lee's last words, "I would rather die a thousand deaths than do what I have to do today," were like a heavy weight on King's shoulders. But, he rationalized, at least he had been assured by General Homma, commander of all Japanese forces in the Philippines, that our 12,000 American and 54,000 Filipino soldiers would be treated with respect and dignity.

We were not. General Homma did not keep his word. Instead, we were told by our captors that we were lower than dogs, and that was the way we would be treated from that day forward. "Like dogs," said our Japanese camp commander. That was our treatment for the next forty months.

It was a humiliating and terrifying experience. As a young American soldier of twenty-one, I had never imagined surrender or being imprisoned. The emotions still rise within me as I vividly remember the hour we laid down our arms. We prisoners were marched without food or water, eighty miles over twelve days in over 108 degrees of unrelenting sun to our first prison, Camp O'Donnell. Sick with malaria, starvation and dysentery, many of us were too weak to lift one foot in front of the other. We soon learned that stopping along the way for any reason meant instant death. Falling down and being unable to get up meant the same punishment. The goal on the march was to keep standing, to do whatever the guards told you to do… if you could figure it out. All their orders were shouted at us in Japanese. Talking to each other was not allowed, so asking another what was said was taboo. My nose was broken, my teeth knocked out and I sustained a deep gash in the head, all because I looked with anger at one of the guards. I saw my fellow soldiers tortured, starved, shot at point-blank range, ridiculed, brainwashed, and beaten. Some were maimed for life. I was forced to watch helplessly as my friend's head was cut off by a Japanese officer wielding a lethal Samurai sword in one swift, brutal decapitation. I saw one of our men buried alive in a ditch alongside the road leading out of Bataan. His screams still echo in my ears.

From those 12,000 Americans who began the march, 7,200 arrived at prison Camp O'Donnell. Once there, we continued dying from the effects of the march at a rate of about fifty men a day. Out of those 12,000 Americans who marched on Bataan, about 1,600 came home alive.

Yet this was not the end of our trials. After four months of starvation and emotional abuse in the prison camp, we boarded the "Clide Maru," one of the unmarked Japanese freighters known as "Hell Ships." With a human cargo of 500 Americans down in the hold, our destiny was to become slave labor for the Mitsui Coal Mining Company in Japan. Of the twenty-three unmarked Japanese ships carrying almost 19,000 POWs, only a little over 8,000 survived the trip. Because the freighters were unmarked, they were prime targets for American submarines or dive-bombers. One of the less fortunate Hell Ships, the "Arisan Maru," was torpedoed by the U.S.S. Shark. Of the 1,800 American POWs on board not killed by the American submarine's torpedoes, those who jumped overboard hoping to swim to safety were targeted and shot by Japanese soldiers. Only nine survived. Our ship was luckier. We only lost twenty-two of our five hundred, and arrived in Japan thirty-four days after leaving Manila.

Yes, I lived on, but only to be forced into slave labor, working twelve hours a day without any pay in a Mitsui-owned coal mine. We suffered day-to-day beatings on starvation rations of rice for three-and-a-half long years. Each day was a challenge. Would the ceiling cave in? Would I be crushed to death by a coal car speeding up the shaft? The fear of death was never-ending.

When freedom finally arrived on August 15, 1945, I celebrated a new beginning of my life. That was the day I became a free man once again, and I was determined to make the most of this gift of liberty.

But my struggles were not yet over. My wife Laura, who I had married while stationed at Fort Knox, Kentucky in 1941, had been told I was "Missing In Action," and presumed dead. She had waited three long years for some word of encouragement from our government, but none came. I returned home, excited to get my life back, only to learn that the love of my life, the woman whose very existence had sustained me and kept me alive during those long years of senseless torture, had married someone else.

I survived that, too.

But there is more to surviving than just being a physical survivor. I had returned home a free man, but I was still imprisoned…a prisoner of my own mind. I was stuck like a record in the same groove, playing the same ghoulish scenes over and over and over. For years, these events colored my existence, seeped into my nightmares, and drained me of energy.

I became aware that something was terribly wrong after about ten years of this stranglehold on my life. What was causing me this inability to enjoy life? The memories of the past came back to haunt me, and my hatred, anger and shame returned full force. I found myself in an even more difficult battle. This was the battle over myself, the self that felt guilty that I lived on, when others had not. I asked myself, "Why, God? Why did I survive, but not my friends and comrades?"

I realized that I was becoming a "delayed casualty." This made me furious. I had evaded those bastards who had tried very hard to kill me during the war. To die now, not to live my life fully again, would mean they ultimately won, and I was just too stubborn to let them win. I wanted my life back. And so, little by little, I consciously changed gears before going over the hill of depression. Thus began the story of how I slowly and deliberately saved my own life.

When I first came home from the war, I spent eighteen months on and off in the hospital just getting my physical health back. I had lost almost half my weight in captivity, going from 185 pounds down to 97. My nose was broken, and my shoulder, hip and back had sustained grievous injuries. It was a long recovery to achieve the full use of my arms and legs, and live a life without constant pain, but I made it.

Lying in that hospital bed gave me a lot of time to think. Was it just luck that I had survived such an ordeal? How much was due to my own thoughts and actions? If a portion of it was due to my making my own luck, could I use these skills to get back my life? I realized that I had unconsciously followed a plan of survival, and those principles that saved my life in captivity were the same principles I could use again to save it. They included things like taking care of my physical needs; reaching out and communicating with others; banishing all negative thoughts and emotions; disciplining myself to strictly maintain a positive attitude; defining each problem and then solving it through setting realizable goals and objectives; then acting on them in small steps; letting go of hatred and bitterness through acceptance of the past and forgiveness. Those are the principles that I followed every day, and they gave me back a life worth living.

Always, the underlying theme was courage, starting with the courage to remember.

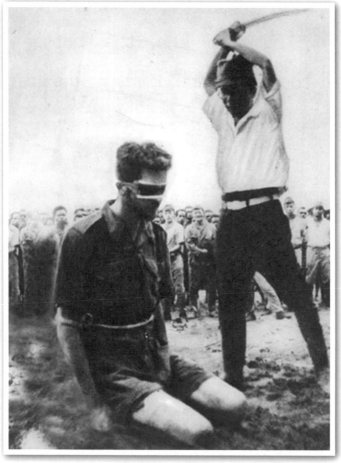

... some will die.

"You shall know the truth,

and the truth shall make you free."

Chapter Two
The Courage to Remember

I thought my suffering would be over when the war ended for us Prisoners of War on August 15, 1945. "From now on," I told myself, "things will be all right." I was going to live, I was going to go home, to see my wife Laura and my parents and four brothers again. I was going to be a free man.

I had no idea what was in store for me.

Now the Real Battle Began

We boarded the U.S. Army Transport ship "Klipfontein" for home. Two army nurses who had been captured and sent to an internment camp for women and civilians in Santo Tomas happened to be on our same ship. It was the first time in over three years I was with a couple of American women, and you can just imagine my excitement. The captain of the ship invited me to take care of the on-board entertainment and to be the editor of the on-board newspaper, along with the help of some other soldiers. With their help as my editorial staff, we named it "Frisco Lookout," and were able to publish an interesting and informative newspaper daily. I was very grateful for something positive to do for the twenty-eight days our journey took.

But my mind was already starting to shatter. As we stood on the deck, watching our ship leave, I started to cry and shake. I was suddenly aware of all the friends I was leaving behind, hundreds who had died or been killed, many on the side of the road out of Bataan, many in the water bombed and strafed by the Japanese on other Hell Ships. I was overcome with emotion.

As long as I was doing something, I was in fine shape. During the day, I had my activities: I had a band in which I played the drums, and I wrote the newspaper. I even had a private beautiful stateroom at the top of the ship. But at night, with nothing to do, when I was alone, that's when I started to shake, to see over and over again all the things I had hoped would leave my mind forever, horrible images I would never forget.

At the time, we didn't have a name for what I was experiencing. I could deal with it during the day when I was active, but at night, I could not sleep at all. I would toss and turn, and be up all night, awake. I had constant visions, not just of things that happened to me, but also the persecutions I had been forced to watch others endure. Vivid visions plagued me night after night.

I particularly remember the one time watching the Japanese perform a water-treatment torture to get information from an American guerrilla they had captured. They laid him down and tied him to a board pitched at a twenty-degree angle, with his head down at the bottom, his feet at the top. They pried his mouth open, as one man poured a little teakettle full of water down his mouth while the other held his nose. He was drowning! The water was going into his lungs, and he had no way to breathe. He was drowning, and I helplessly had to watch this poor man. When the captor took his hand off the American's nose, he belched out all the water, gasping for air. They'd scream at him in Japanese, and then hold his nose, and pour the teakettle of water down his throat all over again. This went on and on and on until the man couldn't take it any longer, and passed out. I don't know if he died then or not. I never saw him after that.

This scene and many others just as terrifying would replay in my mind over and over every single night on the ship going home. It was shocking and horrible, and I couldn't understand why it was happening to me. Although the actual torture was over, I was stuck re-experiencing not only my own anguish, but also everyone else's I had been forced to witness, helpless to stop myself from the flow of unbearable suffering it caused me.

After that first night, the nurses could tell I was suffering. They asked, "What's happening, Lester? What's wrong?" When I told them what I was seeing, what my mind was doing, they said, "We understand." They didn't have to say anything more. They had been in those battles with us. Maybe they hadn't fired any guns, but through taking care of all of us, they knew every detail of what we'd gone through. It was such a comfort to me that they understood. But they were the rare exception.

No one knew about PTSD in those days. No one could tell me that combat veterans almost universally suffer sleep problems. I just knew that it was damaging me. The emotional pain was as excruciating as any physical pain I suffered from the torture I endured at the hands of the Japanese.

On that ship coming home is where I first realized I had a problem, one I didn't know how to define.

What Was My Problem?

In the 1980s, after the men came home from Vietnam, they first gave it a name: Post-Traumatic Stress Disorder. PTSD is a condition characterized by intense fear, helplessness, or horror resulting from the exposure to any extreme trauma, a terrifying event or ordeal in which grave physical harm or death was threatened, anticipated, or actually occurred. Violent personal assaults, natural or human caused disasters, accidents, or military combat all qualify.

When I first heard the name, I rankled at having it called a disorder, having our condition defined as a mental illness. I understood we were stuck in a reaction of horror and helplessness to the traumas we had experienced. But I didn't think it crazy to react this way, considering what happened to us. We needed help, not labels.

Not everybody who goes through a trauma experiences PTSD. Generally people who have prolonged trauma over many years are at greater risk for developing it. The incidence among the general population is around 8%, but the highest rates are found among survivors of rape, military combat and captivity. Up to 20-30% of our combat veterans returning from Afghanistan and Iraq exhibit symptoms.

There are three characteristic sets of symptoms:

- persistent re-experiencing of the traumatic event (nightmares, flashbacks)

- persistent avoidance of any stimuli associated with the trauma, and

- persistent increased arousal, or anxiety.

Typical symptoms include depression, angry outbursts, crying, panic attacks, agoraphobia, difficulty concentrating, anxiety, worrying, disturbed logical thinking, restlessness, nightmares, confusion, irritability, nervousness, extreme loneliness, suicidal thoughts, and breathing difficulties.

You might boil it down to 1) being stuck in the past; 2) avoiding or being unable to enjoy the present; and 3) always being worried about the future. They say if you have these symptoms for more than a month, and they start interfering with your ability to function, you are suffering from this condition.

I was suffering from this condition.

Stress can result from anything that poses a threat or challenge to our well-being. Not all stresses are bad; sometimes the challenge which stress creates within the body results in the necessary energy required to leap into action. For example, imagine witnessing a car overturned on the road ahead. Flames shoot out of the bottom, and you know someone is trapped inside. The stress of seeing this accident causes a rush of adrenalin to be produced in your body, giving you the necessary courage and energy to get the door of that car open and pull the person to safety. This is one scenario where stress can be beneficial.

But some stresses are devastating. PTSD is especially common when you are helpless to do anything, like when, in order to save my own life, I failed to save the life of another. If I had intervened, I would have been killed. I am often asked what was the worst thing I endured as a Prisoner of War. My answer was always the same: the worst thing by far was being forced to watch your friends die, powerless to help them or save them.

The stress was compounded with a sense of guilt. I felt guilty for surviving. I've been fighting that guilt all these years. Only years later did I learn that painful guilt feelings about surviving when others did not, or about the things we had to do to survive, was very common among those of us with PTSD.

Fifty Years of Not Talking About It

We had boot camp to train us for going to war, but there was no boot camp for coming home. No one told us how bad it would be. The worst part was not being able to talk about what I was experiencing with anyone.

I came back home, and lived at my parents' house. I went back to school on the GI Bill, not knowing how I was going to live through every next day. Mainly, I just wanted to forget the past and move on with my life.

It took fifty years before I could talk about the events of World War II, fearful it would awaken within me further memories I wanted to forget. The problem was, I just couldn't talk about what had happened to me, not to anyone at all, and I was becoming increasingly isolated. I didn't want to burden my family. They'd already been through enough, with my being reported "Missing In Action," maybe even dead. I had a brother living in Detroit, but he had his own problems. I had brothers who lived in Chicago, but they had their own families.

I, on the other hand, had no one to talk to. When I came home, all my high school friends were still overseas. I'd enlisted early; they went in later, and were still in the service. The girls I'd known before were all married to those men who wanted to stay out of the service, and could stay out of it if they got married and got their wives pregnant. So, all the girls I knew were not available, the men were in the service, and the woman I had married thought I was dead, and was now remarried and pregnant. I came back devastated.

What about my combat buddies from Company B of the 192nd Tank Battalion? Of the 168 who went overseas, 48 came back. We'd get together once in awhile. One of them would call up and say, "Hey, we're going to get together," and we'd meet at somebody's house, or at a restaurant or a bar. The first time we got together, I learned that a few had committed suicide already.

That was so horrible. They made it all the way through the war, came home, and then couldn't deal with this new society they'd been away from for so many years. It was another loss for me to absorb, after so many.

We started to talk, had a couple of beers, and chatted about what we were doing. This one was going with the Fire Department, that one with the Highway patrol, another took a job with the city. They all had government jobs. I was the only one who'd gone back to school. That was stressful. There I was, going for a bachelor's degree from Northwestern University, and these guys were already making a good living. They weren't interested in my academic training, or how it was opening up my mind. They wanted to talk about football, baseball, girls… but not academics. Slowly, we drifted apart. They say, "A true friend understands where you came from, believes in where you're going, and wants to travel with you." These men had been my friends in combat, but as civilians, we had little in common anymore. That was a different kind of loss for me to bear.

Even with new people I met, I increasingly found they couldn't understand what I had been through. How could they understand when I couldn't even start to talk about it, couldn't adequately express it? I couldn't find words to describe the atrocities we experienced, and no one would have believed me anyway.

I remember one time when I first came home, I went out with my brother and his boss for lunch, and his boss turned to me and asked, "Was it as bad as they say?"

I thought to myself, "Hell, you have no idea how bad it was!" No matter what I said, it would have been too much. People who ask that kind of question are looking for an answer like, "Yeah, it was just as bad as they said. Now, let's get on with our lunch." They pretended to be interested, but they weren't really interested. I think most people do not listen to you trying to understand what you're saying; instead, they listen thinking of how they're going to reply.

For those who had never been in combat, it was particularly hard to explain. People had an unrealistic attitude about what war was all about. Books, the media, the news – they all romanticized war. A lot of people may have been in a war, but not in combat.

Combat is an entirely different situation. Anybody who's been in combat knows the truth. You're looking at someone eye-to-eye and trying to kill him. It's a minute-to-minute struggle to stay alive. It's one thing for the guy who had used a gun before, and spent his youth killing ducks or rabbits. But imagine the soldier whose entire upbringing was based on "Thou Shalt Not Kill," whose family and church impressed him that killing was unacceptable and wrong, but now had to do the very thing he'd been told never to do. Many of us in combat suffered from this "moral injury," and struggled with feelings of guilt for transgressing our moral code.

And how would I explain our surrender? Surrendering was not something you go around bragging about. The Japanese told us over and over that we were cowards and lower than dogs for surrendering. Over time, I think we all started to believe them. We all had a deep underlying sense of shame, even though we had been ordered by our superior officer to surrender.

Then there was the stigma against showing any weakness. We were warriors; "we serve and protect." We weren't trained to open up our hearts and admit to having nightmares and bad dreams. There was a stigma, too, against having a mental condition. Any returning soldier was afraid that disclosing his affliction could curtail his military career, or worse, label him as "sick." In those days, if the Veteran's Administration said, "We want you to see a psychiatrist," your first thought was, "Keep away from me. I have no need for a psychiatrist. Not a damn thing is wrong with me! I know if I see one, it will be in my record: 'This guy's got a problem.'"

But the biggest reason we didn't talk about what happened to us as POWs during the war was that the U.S. government prepared a document for all of us to sign when we came home that said we would not discuss what had happened to us with anyone else without first getting the War Department's permission, subject to court-martial if you failed to get their okay. At the time, MacArthur was rebuilding Japan's economy to create a new democracy capable of resisting the impending threat of Communism in the Far East. Shortly after that, the Peace Agreement of 1951 between the U.S. and Japan further strengthened the ties between our two countries. We wondered why we had to sign this paper, but many felt, "If this is what our government wants, we shouldn't talk about it." We were still honoring the military code. And so for years we kept it inside.

I was so frustrated. Finally, I made a big decision. "Hell," I thought, "no one wants to talk about this, or know anything about it. The reason talk is cheap is that the supply is much greater than the demand. I'm just going to close up, hide, and not say another word."

But, you know? Hiding your thoughts, isolating yourself is not good when you are in pain. Keeping it all inside, hidden from others takes a lot of energy, and creates more burdens on an already heavy heart.

Trust

Not everyone has your best interests at heart. Some people ask questions because they are idly curious, but really don't care. I had one bad experience in a conversation about my role during wartime that made me even more wary of sharing anything. Six men were standing around the room, talking "men talk." I was a newcomer to this group. One of them turned to me, and asked, "Were you in the service, Lester?"

"Yes, I was."

"Really? What branch?"

"I was in the Army."

"Oh, What outfit were you in?"

I didn't volunteer information. I just answered his questions. "Well, I was in the armored 192nd Tank Battalion, attached to the First Armored Division."

You could hear the quiet of the group.

Finally, one of the men said, "Oh? The First Armored Division was in Italy. You say you were in the Philippines?"

"Yes, we were attached to them."

Within weeks there were rumors around that I was a phony. They warned my girlfriend to be careful of me. One of her friends insisted she come to Texas to get away from me for a while. Another had influence in the Veteran's Administration, and actually had my pension stopped for a time, telling them I was a phony. All this happened to me.

Some people are malicious. More than not being interested in your story, they do not have your best interests at heart. Yes, you don't want to be isolated, but before you entrust someone with your story, first be sure they are trustworthy.

Telling My Story

Why bother telling your story? Because you have to talk about it in order to move beyond the nightmares. It took a lot of research, but I finally learned why, and it does make sense to me now. The reason you have to tell your story, tell all of it, is that when you first undergo a traumatic experience, it is lodged in the most primitive part of your brain, the reptilian part that gives you the "fight or flight" adrenalin boost to get you moving and keep you alive. That part of your brain is outside time and space. That's why each time you re-experience the event as a nightmare or flashback, it seems like it's happening now, over and over again. You can't reason with it. In order to get the experience to a place where you can deal with all the many emotions you had, you have to tell it fully.

Combat veterans, and all survivors of traumatic stress, handle their psychological wounds in different ways. The wounds are real, in spite of the fact that there are no outward signs of distress, no blood, no broken bones. I remember the Japanese would let us POWs out of work only if they could see a broken bone or blood. No blood? You were a phony, and had to go to work! Well, our psychological wounds were like that: no blood showing, but still very real to us.

The brain tries to hide these wounds by tucking them into a corner of the brain, and then deny they are there. You think you can fool others into thinking you are fine, through physical gestures like laughing. But deep inside, the real emotions caused by the hidden stress are there, and the body knows better.

These wounds may lie dormant for years, and then suddenly show their ugly heads again. Until then, if the negative feelings are held inside, they can damage our emotions, behavior and physical well-being. It caused me tremendous strain to keep all these emotions bottled up inside. I had pains in my neck, my shoulders, and my arms. For years, I had headaches. Doctors just said it was tension. They probably knew it was more than that, but they didn't want to bother asking me a lot of questions.

The Healing Power of Telling Your Story

I was the youngest of seven children, and it was my older brother Bill who looked out for me when I came home. He could see the situation I was in: no friends, isolated, living at home, my wife remarried while I was gone. In his own way, he was always there to take care of me.

I came back from the war twenty-five years old, but I seemed an old man who'd had a lot of experiences. Other guys my age I met seemed so much younger. Bill could see I had no buddies. Even though he was forty-six years old at the time, he became my buddy, my primary relationship. We'd play ping pong and cards, and sit and talk for hours. He understood what trauma was about, having lost his wife at the young age of twenty-five to a heart attack. Then, a few years before I returned, he lost a leg in an accident in Ohio. Bill got out of his truck to help move a stalled vehicle, when someone banged into his truck, pinning him in between and taking his leg off. Not that it slowed him down. Bill was quite the athlete. Even with his one leg, he managed to play ping pong, and beat me at it all the time! He was a dynamo. He finished a tennis match using his crutch for his missing leg.

Bill sat down with me and said, "Babe, this is the business I think you should get into." He called me Babe because I was the baby of the family. "You've got to go into some business. Here's what I suggest. You should go into the syrup business, because sugar is on ration. No one can get sugar right now. Without sugar, you can't make fountain syrup. So fountain syrup is at a premium. Go down to the sugar ration board, and tell them you know how to make syrup. Here's a book you can read about how to make it. "

Of course, I went down to the ration board and met the head man in charge. I was still in uniform. He looked at me, saw all my ribbons, and said, "Where the hell have you been?"

I said, "I was a POW."

"Really? What do you need?"

I said, "I need 20,000 pounds of sugar so I can make some syrup so I can make a living."

He said, "That's not going to do it. You'll need 100,000 pounds." And he wrote me out a government order for 100,000 pounds of sugar. So all of a sudden I'm in the syrup business! That was Bill for you.

When I first came home, Bill had me up to his apartment and introduced me to a very attractive lady. Suddenly, he said, "I have to leave for awhile, I'll be back later." You can fill in the rest. That's the kind of guy he was. That was Bill.

Mainly, he knew it was important for me to talk about what happened in the war. "What happened? Tell me the story." And he'd sit there, and say, "Oh, my God. What happened after that? How did you feel about that?" I'd share it with him, and he took notes. The amount that was written down was very small, but what he was letting me do was get it off my chest. He loved me, and knew it had to be done. We must have spent about two weeks talking every day, one or two hours at a time. He let me know where I left off until I got through most of it. I guess you'd say he "debriefed" me. I think it was the most important thing he did for me, encouraging me to tell my story to someone who understood and loved me. They say, "The love and understanding of a friend is sometimes more healing than a doctor's prescription." All I can say is: it's true.

Bill only lived another year. He died at age forty-seven of a heart attack. I still have the handwritten notes he took from those talks we had about my war years. He was a great guy, and I'm sorry he died so soon.

Fifty years later, I wrote my first book about my war years, *My Hitch In Hell*, using Bill's notes. It's only since I put those experiences down in writing that I have been able to talk about it openly, and without any concern. I sat down every day for four hours a day, writing. Sometimes I'd write two to five pages, depending on how I felt or where I was in the book. Sometimes I would write only one paragraph in four hours, and cry for the rest of the time. I'd just sit and cry. In my own way, I got a lot of it out of me.

I guess there is no way to fully explain what a person goes through. I can't really explain my feelings, just as you can't explain yours. It was a traumatic experience. That's the whole point. You have to allow yourself to feel all those feelings in order to heal them. Telling your story is just the beginning.

Tenney and his family, circa 1945
Back row: Bunny, Lou, Joe, Bill and Lester
Front row: Lester's Dad and Mother

Chapter Three
Controlling Your Feelings

I thought I was handling things pretty well, but really, I was numb, stuffing all my emotions deep inside, just trying to make all the negative ones go away. Unfortunately, they never went away; instead, they kept building up steam until one day they erupted like a volcano. The explosion knocked me for a loop.

The trigger was seeing an elderly Japanese man walking toward me in downtown Chicago. Suddenly my brain was on red alert. My heart pounding, I took a second look, thinking, "Was that one of our guards from Camp 17? The one we called Donald Duck?"

In camp, we gave all the guards names like Mickey Mouse, Donald Duck, Four Eyes, since we couldn't pronounce their Japanese ones. We'd talk amongst ourselves, saying things like, "Be careful of Four Eyes."

"Yeah, and Mickey Mouse is just as bad."

Every one of us POWs knew exactly who we meant by these nicknames.

One of the Japanese overseers in the mine we called "Sonofabitch." Unfortunately, not long after the day we gave him the name, Sonofabitch learned what it really meant, and the very next time an American POW called him that, he grabbed a pickax and shovel. Screaming, he smacked the poor soldier right in the face with the shovel, and broke his nose and knocked some teeth out, all in a few seconds.

Now I was looking at a man on the street who had the same kind of face, even that same duck-like waddle as Donald Duck. Could it be him? I was so wound up with hatred and rage, I was ready to walk up and punish him like "Sonofabitch" punished that poor soldier in the mine. Suddenly, I caught myself. This man was much too young to have been in Japan in 1944. Shaken, I stopped myself just in time, still looking at him intensely as we passed on the street.

It was the first time I was aware how violent my response was to any reminder of my years as a prisoner, beaten and tortured by Japanese guards and by civilian workers in the mine. It "triggered" all the rage, fear, and hatred I'd had to suppress over those many years. Had I shown any hatred or anger while working in the mine or in camp 17, I would have been tortured and killed. And now, I realized I had to be careful again, or I might kill an innocent man walking down the street, and end up in jail for the rest of my life. I was stunned. I tried to shrug this emotion off, but it was becoming increasingly clear I was fighting a serious battle.

I'm sorry to say these "triggers" never completely go away. You just learn to know them better. Even in Japan as a visitor many years later, every time I saw an older Japanese man on the street, I still wondered, "Where were you during the war?" It still brought back those memories.

Adding Insult to Injury

Any insolent remark that made me feel small was another trigger that would set me off. I remember my first date with a young lady, going for dinner and dancing at the Palmer House Hotel in downtown Chicago. As I pulled up to the entrance to drop off my date and the car, the driver of a truck behind me started leaning on his horn. He stuck his head out the window, and hollered, "Hey jerk, move it!"

Did I hear that? Did he actually call me "jerk?" My mind was racing. Suddenly my body was back in Camp 17, thrashed by the guards who were screaming in Japanese we were "cowards, lower than dogs." It wasn't only the physical torture, as much as the mental abuse that demoralized us. I swore to myself, "If I ever get out of this alive, no one will ever talk that way to me again." So when that truck driver called me a "jerk," it triggered my brain.

Jerk, he called me. No one was ever going to insult me again. You don't call me a jerk! I was called all kinds of things by the Japanese guards, when I had to take it. But now, I don't. In fact, I won't.

I got out of my car, walked over to the truck driver's side, leaned in, took his keys out of the ignition, and, making a few choice comments to him reflecting my state of mind, threw his keys as far away as I could throw them. He may still be looking for them.

Liar

Another example of what could trigger that rage happened several years later when I was a student at Northwestern University. I hadn't graduated high school when I enlisted in 1940. Years later, when I came home from the war, I went back to school on the GI Bill. Because of the mass of new young men wanting an education, most universities approved 100% of the applicants without any reservations. I was now in my mid-twenties, so I enrolled in Northwestern, and they accepted me right away. After I was there for about two years, the Dean of the College of Business called me into his office. Since all my grades had been fine, I had no idea what he wanted.

He said, "Mr. Tenney, you lied to us."

That was a trigger. You don't call me a liar. I took his desk in both hands, lifted it, and shoved it on top of him. "You bastard," I said, "don't you ever call me a liar!"

He looked at me and said, "You signed a paper saying you graduated from high school, and you never did."

I replied, "The paper I signed said, 'High school last attended.' And if you don't know that definition, what right do you have to be sitting there talking to me?"

The Dean called his secretary. "Bring in Mr. Tenney's application." He read it. It said, "high school last attended." I said, "I last attended Lane Tech."

He apologized. But the damage had already been done.

I can be called many things by many people, and during the war, they called me many things, and I just had to take it. But you don't call me a liar now that I'm a free man, living in this free country.

Never Show Any Emotion

At no time during our captivity could we ever show any emotions, not to our captors, not even to our fellow soldiers. You didn't want your buddy to know you were crying, so you kept it all inside. You had to go on with your life. You didn't know when you would be released, if ever. One year? Two years? Ten years? That was the problem. If you knew you had to serve a certain amount of time, you could look forward to getting out.

But not knowing when, or if – that was the hard part. Would we ever get out? Would I live until tomorrow morning? No one knew. Everyone had to live with that same uncertainty.

Even if the Americans were victorious, we were uncertain if our lives would be saved or spared. Prime Minister/Army Minister Tojo had given orders to kill all Allied POWs and captives the minute the Americans landed on Japanese soil. In 1944, when the Japanese held the Philippines, they considered it "Japanese soil." Accordingly, when the Americans sought to retake it, the Japanese massacred all but eleven of the POWs in the Palawan prison camp. We desperately feared our fate might be the same.

We simply couldn't exhibit any emotion. Even when the war was over, we didn't know how much emotion we could show. American fighter planes flew over Camp 17 in July, 1945, dipping their wings as if to wave to us, and then flew on to strafe the Japanese. Even then, we had a horrible time trying to figure out if we should show sorrow, or if we could feel free to jump up and down, screaming, "Hurray!"

Freedom to Choose

But that was then, and now was now. I was a free man, and that meant I was free to choose how I was going to live, and how I was going to react to any threat, real or imagined. During those long war years, I was a victim; now, I was a survivor. But I would only call myself a true survivor if I were no longer a victim. So I made a big decision: to take back control of my well-being and my destiny. If I looked to blame anyone, I'd have to blame myself, for I was the one in charge of my life.

I knew I had to do something. My emotions were being triggered by reminders of the past, and I could tell my feelings were completely out of control. The amount of energy I was releasing was not in proportion to the event. Some guy honks his horn and calls me a jerk. Did that justify the amount of anger I paid out, throwing his keys to God knows where?

I had to be more aware of what was causing my emotional explosions. After all, how could I solve a problem if I didn't first know what it was? I had to understand what specific threats would hook me. I had to identify each one with a name or a number, and prioritize each in importance so I could come up with a way to manage them. Not everything had the same importance. Which were the ones I could laugh off or ignore? Seeing a Japanese person, for example, that was a minor trigger, a #1, manageable. But somebody ridiculing me, embarrassing me, or hollering at me was a #10. It was very difficult now to ignore any abuse to my sense of self, after all those many years when I couldn't do anything but bow to it.

Becoming aware of these things about myself, experiencing those feelings I had stuffed for so long, and understanding the damage that had been done to me was hard, but it put me back in control. I could name my triggers. I could think, "Oh, this person just did a #9 on me, 'calling me a name.' How am I going to respond in a way that isn't: 'shoot him?'"

Choosing Differently

Even as a prisoner of the Japanese, though I lost control of so many physical freedoms, I never lost control over my thoughts and attitude. I remember thinking, "How can I solve this problem when they say these things to me? How can I control myself and not strike back when they beat me, knowing that if I do, I'm dead?" The only answer then was: show no emotion. Stuff it.

But now, back in America, I was having the same problem. And I didn't want to stuff my feelings anymore. I didn't want to place things on the back burner. So what could I do when someone insulted me, called me a liar, a phony?

Here's the strange thing. I'd still get angry. But after looking at all the things that triggered me, giving them names and numbers, deciding which were important and which were not, after understanding what was really causing all that anger, fear, pain and uncertainty, and letting all those feelings out of the bag, suddenly it didn't seem so important anymore to act on those feelings. It was enough just to feel them again.

CHAPTER FOUR
The Power to Choose

I know what you're thinking. You're wondering, "How is 'doing nothing' different from 'putting all your feelings on the back burner?'" Here's the difference: Everyone occasionally numbs themselves to make bad feelings go away, and I was no exception. Stuffing my feelings was all I could do for a long time just to get me through the days. There are plenty of ways to do it; my drug of choice at the time was alcohol.

Those first few months, I was an unhappy young man. I had no friends at home. The men had gone into the service much later than I did, and they were still overseas. The young ladies I used to know were all married and pregnant, and my wife, the girl of my dreams all those years I was away, was now married to someone else. My right arm didn't work right, and my left one was still sore from a bayonet wound of many years past, even after an operation and further care at the Army hospital. I weighed about 135 pounds, and had little if any strength in my arms, back or legs. I was a basket case.

I hadn't been discharged from the hospital yet, but they let me take a leave from time to time. One thing the doctors never did during that long eighteen-month convalescence: they never stopped me from taking time off and just getting out of there. They knew better than to say, "I'm sorry, Mr. Tenney, but you can't leave the hospital." I might have broken a window just to escape. "Oh, yeah? Watch me!"

There was a time when, during one of these breaks back home, I would go to the local bar every night after dinner. Since I was still in the service, and wearing my uniform, everyone wanted to buy me a drink. It wasn't long before I was pretty souped up. I'd sit at the bar and play "Twenty-Six" with the girl at the dice box, who I called the Bar Lady. For this game, you'd get ten dice in a cup, and ten rolls. I'd sit there and roll the dice. Call a number, any number. Six. I'd roll the dice. If your number came up twenty-six times in ten rolls, you'd get a drink. That's the game. I'd play all night. At the end of the evening, the Bar Lady would drive me to her house, put me to sleep, wake me in the morning, make me breakfast, and drive me home. This went on for about two weeks.

My mother and dad thanked her each time she dropped me off. Of course, they could tell that the Bar Lady was about fifty years old, and they were starting to worry we might be getting serious. What my family didn't realize was I had nothing else going on. The only people I knew, my whole social life, was in that bar. My parents tried to solve my problem by inviting me to their friends' houses. But I wanted to be with people I could relate to. My parents' friends were so much older, leading very subdued lives. I knew that wasn't going to work.

One morning when the Bar Lady got me home, I entered the house, and found my dad sitting up, rocking in his chair.

He greeted me, and then asked quietly, "Babe, what did I do wrong?"

He was taking the blame for what I was doing! Suddenly, I saw what my actions were doing to my dad. I felt like the roof had just caved in. My hurt was mine, and mine alone. I didn't want to hurt anyone else with my actions, especially my dad. I knew something had to change, right then. I decided to get my life back in order, and from that day on, I stopped drinking. That was my job, and no one could do my work for me. I never went back to the bar.

So many of us who have lived through a severe trauma don't want to feel any emotions. Why would you? You've just survived something beyond horrible. We're comforted as long as we're numb. And society is more than happy to help us avoid those memories. "Have another drink," my friends at the bar would say. "You've earned it." Or the doctors might say, "Here, take this pain medication. It will help you get through the day."

But the unfortunate truth is just suppressing these emotions doesn't make them go away. It just silences them for a time, until the alcohol or the drugs wear off, when those feelings rear their ugly heads again full force. Some memory will trigger them, and then all that stuff will come up all at once. And you'll shoot somebody or wind up in jail because you overreacted, because you haven't learned to control yourself.

That's why I say it takes courage to remember. When you tell your story, it's going to bring up all these emotions. Well, let them come. Feel them fully. They'll pass. You don't need to react. That's how you become the master of that feeling; it's no longer the master of you.

We can't keep pushing those feelings away, because it's only by feeling all of them that we live life to the fullest. Otherwise, we just put our lives on hold.

Training Your Mind

I was tutored in the power of the mind and the mastery of one's thoughts from the story of my birth. My parents were two of the most positive individuals I've ever known. I was the youngest of seven children, two of whom died in a freak accident in 1918 before I was born, the only two daughters my parents had. They loved those two girls dearly, and grieved their loss. But after the family doctor suggested they try to have another child, they never looked back. They were my living example of how to survive through personal fortitude and a positive attitude. I was born out of that catastrophe. As much as they loved their only daughters, at no time did they ever express they were sorry that I, their newborn child, was a boy. They never looked back.

When I look back on my days growing up, I only remember a house filled with love. I grew up during the Depression, and yet we never thought of ourselves as poor; we just didn't have any money. Because we didn't think of ourselves as poor, there was always enough to go around. Every Christmas, Easter and Thanksgiving we'd pack up my father's company truck with baskets filled with food for all our neighbors who were needy. My parents were a living example of how you can choose to think about yourself and your circumstances.

I remember when I was about fifteen, my father said, "You have the ability to do anything you want. Just make up your mind what it is, and you can do it." He made me see that I was strong —not just physically, but also mentally. He said, "You have to train your mind. And you have to believe in yourself, that you can accomplish anything you set out to do."

He didn't say it would be easy, though. He said I'd have to work hard at whatever I wanted. Like the old saying, he believed "the only place 'success' comes before 'work' is in the dictionary."

The Power of Positive Choices

Probably the most important thing my father said to me was when I was about seventeen. I was going out with a group of kids who were not exactly the best. One night, Dad said, "You know, I think it would be nice if you start to go with a group of people you could learn from, instead of those you have to teach."

What a profound statement. He made me understand I could learn from the people I chose as my friends. I turned this thought over in my mind for several weeks. I had never before considered I had the power to choose the people with whom I spent my time, and I had no idea how important it would be in shaping — and ultimately saving — my life.

When the draft for the war began, I knew that not only would I be required to go, but that being young and healthy, I would be drafted right away. Putting Dad's concept into practice, I decided to go out and find a National Guard unit that had the leadership and positive individuals with whom I would be proud to serve, and enlist in that one. I went to three or four National Guard units, but it wasn't until I saw an article in the *Chicago Tribune* written by a Sergeant Danca that I felt hopeful.

In the article, Sergeant Danca wrote how proud he was to serve his country, and signed it with the name of his unit, the 192nd Tank Battalion, Company B. I thought, "Those are the kind of people I want to be with." I went to visit, and enlisted with them that very day. Making that choice undoubtedly saved my life, because the loyalty and sacrifices we soldiers made for each other kept us alive through our darkest hours.

To this day I am grateful for my buddies Bronge and Cigoi who sacrificed their own comfort and safety to make sure I survived the Bataan Death March. I was brutally injured by a Japanese guard swinging his Samurai sword as he rode by on horseback, when the end of his blade hit my left shoulder and missed my head and neck by inches. Bronge and Cigoi called the medics from the rear to sew me up, and then carried me, putting their arms under my armpits. They didn't let me fall, which in those circumstances would have meant my certain death.

Another soldier who saved my life was Bob Martin. We were together in prison Camp 17 in Japan, working the Mitsui coal mine. After being badly injured in the mine, Bob was assigned kitchen duty, serving rice to the rest of us. That's all we had to eat all day, one small Bento box of rice. We could barely exist on that, working twelve-hour shifts underground in the heat. All of us POWs were dying of starvation, and for my crime of trading American-made products to the Japanese for cigarettes, and then trading the cigarettes for food, I was condemned to be executed. How I got myself out of that is a whole different story, but in the end, my life was spared. I was confined instead to a tiny cell in the *esso* (guardhouse) for ten days, and had to survive on one half cup of water and one half ration of rice a day for the duration. It was Bob Martin who personally took it upon himself to see that I got a little bit more rice every day. He knew I had to have more food to live, so every time he came into my cell, he filled my Bento box to the very top with rice, packing it down to get as much in as possible. Had he been caught, he would have been killed. In spite of that, he took that risk to save my life.

Bob and I remained very close friends for the rest of his life. I was very sad when he died.

An Attitude of Gratitude

I came out of the war with the knowledge that I'd never be able to choose how or when I would die. But I also learned I would always be able to choose how I was going to live. You can't adjust the wind; you can only adjust the sails. Even as a prisoner, I could choose my attitude and my thoughts. I could spend my time feeling sorry for myself, or be grateful for those people who saved my life. I chose to be grateful.

I trained my mind to look for the seed of goodness in every situation. This is not easy, especially given the horrible circumstances we've experienced. At first, everything seems black. But if you stick with it, you'll be surprised to find something good in everything you thought was 100% bad. It might be only a small thing, like "it could have been worse." But the good is there, I promise you. You just have to look long enough.

In my case, I never knew how strong I really was, or that I could overcome the adversities I had to face. Along the way, I've enjoyed deep and lasting friendships that many others never have in their lifetimes. Because of what happened to me, my whole outlook on what's important in life changed. It made me look for reasons why I had survived, which gave me a renewed sense of purpose and direction. Who knows if I would have gone into teaching or pursued a PhD if I hadn't had those experiences? Most of all, I learned how forgiveness could turn me from a victim to a true survivor.

Psychologists call this way of thinking "Cognitive Behavioral Therapy." This approach teaches people they cannot control every aspect of the world around them; however, they can control how they deal with things and events by actively choosing how they think and feel about them. I think it's more than a therapy. To be effective, it has to become a way of life, as instinctive as breathing. I've had to live with my memories every day now for over seventy years. The power of choosing is the way I've become grateful for every one of them.

"In life, if you don't risk anything, you risk everything."

Chapter Five
Love Was Just a Four-Letter Word

One of the most important things a person who suffers from serious trauma can do is be with people who care about him. To all outward appearances, ten years after the war's end, it appeared that I had done so. I had remarried and started a family. But somehow, I didn't feel fulfilled.

I always was working, although it seemed I had an endless series of jobs. Luckily, making a living was always easy for me, since working was like therapy. I loved accomplishing what I was challenged to do. Whatever job I undertook, I persevered, and did well. You could say we were getting by financially. But I moved from job to job, never happy with any of them.

Why? What was the reason I couldn't stay at one good job, but had to leave and go on to another? I was making good money, but would suddenly leave it to pursue something else. Why was I so restless all the time?

The problem was on the inside. It was one of the lowest points of my life. Like so many of us who suffer from severe trauma, I felt isolated and alone. I had never really recovered from the shock of losing my first wife Laura when she remarried. Then, one year after I returned home, my father died very suddenly. Shortly after, my brother Bill passed away quite unexpectedly. Three horrible losses. Yes, I had remarried, but it was more on the rebound than anything else. While recovering from my war injuries at Schick General Hospital in Iowa right after the war's end, I met a fellow soldier also from Chicago. I was dating a Red Cross worker I thought he should meet, while he wanted me to meet his sister. Ironically, he wound up marrying the girl I had been dating, and I married his sister! But I married for all the wrong reasons, thinking I could replace my family with hers, only to fill up an empty heart. I was just going through the motions of my life, not really living it. For me, love was just a four-letter word.

Of course, looking back on it now, I can see I was unhappy with everything. My loneliness was profound. I didn't feel loved or understood or important to anyone in my new wife's family. In fact, I felt like a second-class citizen all those years. My father-in-law never invited me to go with all the rest of the family to brunch every Sunday. I don't ever remember my in-laws ever calling me by my name. I felt invisible, a stranger in my own home, low man on the totem pole, carrying the weight of the world on my shoulders. I didn't feel like anyone really cared whether I lived or died.

Some people might say I was severely depressed, and they probably would be right. So many of us who suffer from traumatic stress appear to be coping, but feel only pain. A part of me could understand how some of my buddies who survived the war came home, only to commit suicide, just to stop that pain. But that wasn't like me. I would never, ever do something like that.

The one shining light in my life was my son, the apple of my eye. He was sharp, smart, just an all-round good kid. He loved swimming and outdoor camping, and I loved him dearly. He was stuck in the middle of our unhappy family, and that was the worst of it. In my day, people stayed together, living lives of quiet desperation "for the sake of the kids." I did that for nine years.

I began to see that sacrificing my own happiness for the sake of others was a pattern in my life. It seemed like I had spent my whole lifetime pleasing others, appeasing my platoon leader or company commander, my Japanese captors just to stay alive, and now, appeasing my wife and her family, doing what they wanted when they wanted. I had been a puppet all those years, moving this way and that at the pull of the string, keeping others happy at the expense of myself.

What about my own happiness? I had gone through enough heartache, done my hitch in hell and survived. What had I survived for, if my life held no promise of happiness or pleasure? I needed to have some joy in my life, too, but it seemed the only one who cared for me was me. If I wanted happiness, I'd have to take action on my own behalf, and unfortunately the price for that would be high.

My wife and I separated, and only then did I see the damage we were inflicting on our son before my very eyes. We were tearing him apart. He loved us both, and he was being punished. It was like my worst nightmares on the boat coming home, nightmares of watching my fellow prisoners being tortured while I had to stand by helplessly, unable to make it stop. I couldn't let this happen to the one human being I loved most in the world.

Making Tough Choices

A national office machine company had contacted me. Would I manage their office in either San Diego, or Seattle? "Take your pick," they said.

All of a sudden, I was faced with one of the most critical decisions of my life. If I left Chicago, I'd be leaving not only my son, but also my few friends, and many buddies from the war, the entire history of my life up to now. That was my whole support system. I struggled to think what would be the greatest good for everyone concerned, the positives versus the downsides. Like the old carpenter's saying, I needed to "Measure twice; cut once."

I was worried I'd make the wrong choice, not knowing all the consequences beforehand. It looked like all the options had bad consequences. But if I made no decision, would another opportunity like this ever come along again?

No choice was going to be perfect. There are many ways of going forward, but only one way of standing still. Up to now, I was immobilized in inaction. If I wanted a different outcome, I had to move forward. It felt like I was bleeding to death, like my life was bleeding away. "You have to stop the bleeding," life was saying to me, "or you will die."

On a bleak day in March, I left Chicago, left my son to live with his mother, left him with a brief explanation, a "goodbye," a hug and a kiss. I left with the hope that this very hard decision would prove right for him and for all of us over time. An unhappy home was no place to be raised. I wanted to give my son a chance to grow up in a loving family. I was leaving for his sake.

I got into the car and drove away. The emotion of leaving so much of me behind, of leaving my son, worrying what effect this decision would have, caused me such distress, I cried all the way to California.

I had to take charge and stop worrying. I had made my choice, and now it was up to me to make a go of it. I had to look forward to the challenge ahead of me, and make something of this opportunity. No one else could do it for me. Like they always say, "When you reach the end of your rope, tie a knot in it, and hang on."

Ninety People in Ninety Days

Not quite a week later, I arrived in San Diego, a small sleepy town with a strong Spanish heritage and the presence of Navy and Marine personnel everywhere I went. Since I didn't know a soul in this new place, on that first day, I made a decision: to meet ninety people in ninety days. I needed to know if I could recreate a life for myself, a circle of business contacts and possible friends. I would take them to lunch, get to know them. That's the only way I could know if there was a community that would make this move work. If I could meet that goal, I would stay. If not, I would go to Seattle.

I didn't know it then, but research now shows that for those of us who suffer from trauma, one of the key factors in recovery and resilience is a network of supporting friends and family who understand, and care about you without judging your past. That was the missing piece in the puzzle back in Chicago. Being with people – any people -- causes the release of chemicals in your brain that make you feel better. San Diego was a fresh start, and I instinctively knew this was what I had to do.

I looked for ways I could be proactive to accomplish this goal by looking through the Sunday newspaper for activities to participate in. Lo and behold, the Jewish Community Center was holding auditions for actors in a play called "The Monkey's Paw" at 3:00 p.m. that very day. That would be a good way to meet people, I thought, so I went over and signed up. Within a few minutes, I met five or six other people who were also auditioning. As luck would have it, I got a lead role. More importantly, I met five or six people who were candidates for a lunch date later in the week. Making my goal was off to a good start.

One of the women in the play invited me to fill in as a fourth in a bridge game. Seems there was a young lady who had recently been divorced who needed a partner to play. Would I be interested in joining? Three tables of bridge meant eleven other people to meet, which was my goal. Quickly, I agreed. What this person didn't know was that I had never played bridge before in my life. Would I let that stop me? Never.

I've always believed that life is 10% what happens to you and 90% what you make of it. I knew I had been isolated and lonely in Chicago, and that had contributed to my deep unhappiness. I had to find ways to connect to other people, whether it felt comfortable or easy. People were my lifeline.

Bridge I could learn.

Fake It Until You Can Make It

My partner's name was Betty. I went to her home to meet her several days before we were to play, and she told me she had just taken a course in advanced bridge using Goren's methods. "I have all my notes on index cards," she said.

I couldn't help but notice how beautiful Betty was. "Oh, that's great," I said. "Do you mind if I look at them?"

"Not at all. In fact, you can borrow them," she offered.

I spent the next couple of days memorizing all the index cards. Luckily, I had played some cards before, and had a good card sense. Unfortunately, the card games I played had only included Poker and Hearts. But that was okay. I had a very good memory, and always enjoyed a challenge. I proceeded to memorize every single one of those index cards to prepare for our game.

The evening of the game arrived, and Betty presented me to her friends with a warm introduction. "I would like you to meet Lester Tenney," she said. "He just came in from Chicago." I felt a rush of gratitude to be included in her group of close friends, hopeful I would finally find my place at last.

We were going to play duplicate bridge, which meant we would be competing against the other two couples in the same position as us at the other two tables. As we sat down to play, I told the others at our table, "I might be a little slow. It's been a long time since I've played." I didn't tell them how long!

"That's fine," they said. They seemed friendly.

Betty was picking up her cards, and I glanced over at her. She was smiling, and I was feeling something new inside. I was hoping she would like me. Picking up my cards one at a time, I arranged them by suit. I saw that they were waiting for me to say something, and realized I had the first bid. The pressure was on. I mentally went through the index cards in my mind, thinking through everything I had learned over the past few days. From those notes, I realized I had enough points in my hand that I could say an opening bid. "One club," I said. My mind was alert and racing, listening for any cues that would help me out so I wouldn't look like a complete fool.

Betty's turn to bid, she smiled and said, "One heart." She was asking with her eyes, did I have any heart support for her?

Did I ever.

I was able to survive that whole evening, playing bridge for the first time. More than that, I felt challenged, and that made it fun. That's another thing I didn't know: learning a new skill creates its own reward by releasing those chemicals in your brain that give you a feeling of well-being, a feeling of having fun. Fun! What a concept.

But what was really fun was watching Betty expertly play the game. She responded so sweetly, so charmingly, smiling and joking about life, a lady throughout. As I looked at her, I realized I was feeling affection, the return of pleasure.

On the way home she said how much she enjoyed having a partner again, and complimented me on how well I had done that evening. We had come in second place. Not bad for an amateur! As we laughed together, sharing the excitement of winning, I realized what I had been missing all those years in Chicago was a partner, a true partner. My excitement was never important to my wife or her family. When I was down, or when things didn't work out for me, no one in my household had any empathy. This is what I had been seeking: a partner, someone with whom I could share life's ups and downs. My whole life had been like the only card games I knew, games of competition: "I win; you lose." How enjoyable to play a game where your partner supported you, where your high cards could support their low ones, where their strength together was what mattered. I liked this game. I liked this concept of partnership.

She said she hoped we would be able to play again. I asked if I could come over the following evening and take her out to dinner so I could learn more bridge. She countered, "Why don't you come over and share our dinner, and I'll teach you more about it?"

For the next week, I had dinner with Betty and her boys every single night. It was the highlight of making San Diego my home. By the end of the week, we knew each other pretty well. We told each other our life stories, and as I responded to her questions about me and my family, I could tell she was interested in every word by her eyes, her hand gestures, and her casual remarks. I had never experienced this depth of sharing with someone. She made it easy, even when I talked about the hardest things I had had to endure. By Saturday, I suggested we all go out for dinner, and the boys were excited to go out.

After that week, I knew this was someone very special, not just beautiful, but also charming, fun to be with, and a perfect lady. She was in a class all by herself. I wanted to spend the rest of my life with this lady.

Love Is More Than a Four-Letter Word

I knew Betty was the right partner for me for several reasons. One was, she made me laugh. That may sound like a low priority for a decision that will impact your whole life, but for me it was key. For me, humor is a way of putting life in perspective, a basic survival tool. They say it's the best medicine, especially if we can laugh at ourselves. Suddenly, I was laughing at all the crazy jokes we would play on each other. Up to then, the only feelings I had were sadness and loss, fear and anger, worry, and determination. I hadn't laughed in so long, or felt pleasure, or anticipation, or excitement. No wonder I felt dead inside. I hadn't laughed in such a long, long time.

Secondly, she made me want to be the best person I could be, to reach my highest potential. They say that success in marriage is not so much a matter of finding the right person as it is in being the right person, and I wanted to be that person for Betty and her boys. I wanted it for my boy, too. I knew that the years ahead would be painful for him, but maybe through being a part of a loving family I could reach out to him in the future as a better, stronger role model of what a happy marriage could look like.

What I discovered from playing that bridge game was as true about Betty in our life together as at the card table. Whenever we are together, there is an unspoken message between us. I am able to share how much I care for her, and how much I trust her decisions. She, in turn, has always given a helping hand in everything I do, and showed respect for my opinions. We have give and take on both sides, and plenty of love. Because of this, we have a true partnership that has flourished over time.

Betty has touched my life with kindness and understanding, and given me what I needed and missed all those many years. She gave me a reason to go on living, and meaning to my life.

Love is the only thing we can take with us when we go, and it makes the end so much easier for both. It is truly life's greatest gift. If you have love, you have it all.

Les and Betty Tenney, married in 1960… the start of a new life

"When it comes to going after what you love in life, don't take 'no' for an answer."

Chapter Six
Dreams and Goals

If you're going to survive, at some point your rational brain has to take over from the "fight or flight" part. You have to use the part of your brain that controls language and the ability to think logically. First, you must imagine a way to survive; then, how to execute that plan. As a prisoner, those skills of planning and setting goals became habitual, a way of thinking. When I came home, I continued using them to attack my problems, and over time, my symptoms settled down and stopped interfering with my life.

I always enjoyed being challenged as a kid, but as a prisoner of the Japanese, the challenge was daily and for much higher stakes. I was constantly on the alert for the next life-threatening crisis. We never knew what might happen in the next ten seconds. It was that unpredictable. You could never be complacent, because if you let your guard down, you might die. My body was always saying, "Be careful! Watch out!"

Today, they call this state "hyper-vigilance." Unfortunately, many of us survivors can't turn it off when we come home. We sit with our backs to the wall in restaurants just to ensure we'll see everyone coming in the door.

It uses a tremendous amount of energy to be always watchful and aware. My post-survival strategy was to use that energy to do something positive, such as finding opportunities to accomplish my dreams.

Hopes, Dreams and Goals

A dream is what you hope will happen, a clear vision of what you want, something to aim for. It's what keeps you going, what makes life worth living. My only problem with the word "dream" is that it's passive. It gives you a feeling of having some power over your destiny, but without action, a dream just stays an idea. I prefer the word "goal." A goal is a dream with a plan and a deadline. When a dream is turned into a goal, you can take a thought and turn it into reality.

I remember how important this attitude was on the Bataan Death March. We were limping, straggling, with no notion where the Japanese were taking us. My friends all around me were being beaten and killed, their bodies left on the road. I knew it was only a matter of time before the same thing would happen to me unless I had a survival plan and a goal to achieve it. There's no point in carrying the ball if you don't know where the goal is; my goal was to get home to my wife Laura. That was my dream. But I couldn't just stand there and dream. In fact, if you rested, you died. To survive, I had to break down my goal into small, attainable steps. I told myself I was going to make it to the next bend in the road. When I got that far, I'd say to myself, "Come on, Les, you can make it to the herd of the caribou in the distance." Always I kept the dream alive of returning to Laura. My dream kept me going, but the goals made it all possible.

Small Steps On a Ladder

Don't try to accomplish everything all at once; life is difficult enough as it is. I didn't set myself a goal like, "I've got to get to the top of that mountain." That's too overwhelming; I would be too discouraged to even take the first step. It's not realistic. You have to break it up into little steps, like counting the number of switchbacks on a trail, and then checking them off a mental checklist as you pass each one.

One of the biggest problems I had with PTSD when I came home was controlling my anger, particularly the inappropriate expression of anger to what triggered it. I used this method to accomplish my goal of controlling my anger by breaking it into a sequence of smaller attainable goals. The first step was to find out what was causing this reaction. The next step was to identify and name each trigger that set me off. Then I assigned it a numerical value from 1 – 10 to describe how intensely each one made me react. The next step was to think of a different, more reasonable way to respond. The next time a #9 "verbal abuse" happened, I'd have something better to say. It's important to design each step to lead up to the final summit. The goal, in this case, was managing my anger acceptably.

I know this sounds like a lot of work, and it is. There's no way around it. But the upside is keeping busy with mental challenges is a great distraction from our suffering. Staying busy mentally is good medicine. With persistence and hard work, your dreams unfold and are fulfilled.

On the Death March, my reward for achieving my goals was another day of life. After I returned home, my rewards were all the ways I learned to channel my negative emotional energy into meaningful pursuits.

Finding My Life's Work

Being with Betty and the boys gave me a new perspective on my work. Suddenly I had people who cared about me, and my work took on the additional meaning of supporting those I loved.

Why was I always changing jobs? Part of it was that I was unable to stop being vigilant and worrying about the future. But the other part had to do with enjoying a continual challenge. When I first started a job, I'd be excited about the problems to solve; but once I solved them, there was no follow-up challenge. Yes, I was always making money, good money. But it was predictable and safe, and I was bored. This may sound strange, but as a Prisoner of War, I had to live at a constant level of alertness and awareness, and to win the "Battle of Life or Death" was exhilarating. You get accustomed to living at that level, and when I came back to a quieter, safer life, it was a difficult adjustment.

Many years later at the age of forty-six, I was surprised when my cardiologist said, "Les, you have a problem with your heart. You're going to have to do something else, or you'll die from the stress." It was the first time in twenty years I had the opportunity to step back and take a hard look at the work I had chosen to pursue.

I had never finished high school. When I was in my senior year, there was no place for me to go. I wasn't going to be able to go to college; my parents didn't have enough money to send me to Northwestern, and that was the only university in our area. Also, in the 1940s, schools had a 10% quota on how many Jewish students they could admit. If Northwestern accepted 120 students that year, only twelve could be Jewish. I wasn't a high enough achiever in high school to qualify. So why not make a few bucks and get married? I was seventeen years old.

Later, in prison camp, trying to put my life in order, I had a lot of time to think about what I wanted to do when I got home. My first thought was, "I want to teach." I wanted to get my education. I don't know where that idea came from, but it was a strong certainty that came from a very deep part of me.

After the war and remarrying, my new family put a lot of emphasis on education, so that was an additional motivation for me to get my college degree. Her father was a lawyer, her brother was a lawyer and a CPA, so when I was accepted at Northwestern on the GI Bill, I enrolled in the College of Business. Had it not been for her, I probably would have pursued Liberal Arts. My forte was my creative side, writing, acting, editing the newspaper, playing the drums in a band. But, I wound up in the College of Business, and it affected the rest of my life. Most of my subsequent jobs were entrepreneurial or in sales.

My war injuries suffered greatly from the cold weather in Chicago, so we wound up moving to Miami. I continued my education in the College of Business at the University of Miami. Then, a funny thing happened. My senior year, I decided to buy property and a house for $8000. The man who owned the company and the land was a friend of mine. He drove up with a truck filled with lumber and everything needed to build the house, delivered it to the lot, and promptly went bankrupt. So now all the money I had in the world was tied up in that lot with no house on it, just a huge pile of raw materials.

I went to the Dean of the Business school and said, "I'm going to have to drop out of school. I have to build a house."

He said, "Lester, you don't have to do that. Change your major to Education and take a course in woodworking. We have some wonderful teachers who will help you." I did what he said. I took all the courses in education, and did my student teaching at Miami Senior High, teaching bookkeeping and business law.

I also enrolled in Woodworking, and just as the Dean said, the woodworking teachers not only helped me, they got all my fellow students involved. At the first meeting of the class, the teacher said, "We're going to be doing something different this year; we're going to learn to build a house." They built my house! The meetings took place at my lot, and the teacher showed us how to put the trusses up, how to put up the side walls, everything. It was amazing. The house was finished by the end of the semester. The next semester I registered for the advanced course. In that one, everyone was required to make a piece of furniture for my house! I wound up with beds, tables, and everything I needed, all made by the students in those two semesters of Woodworking. All because the Dean advised me to change my major.

The funny thing about this story is that in changing my major to build my house and get my degree, life conspired to help me get a taste of what my intuition had desired: to be a teacher. I never had a job so fulfilling, so demanding, so creative and different every day as teaching those high school students at Miami Senior High.

My joy was short-lived. My wife did not like Miami. She missed her family back in Chicago. I went back to a business career, having my own successful income tax service, first in Miami for a series of drugstores, and then in Chicago for all the employees of one of the largest drug companies in the world. All my clients were happy with my work, and wanted my services the next year, but I went on to the next challenge at the next job, and the next, and the next. The truth was, my heart wasn't in any of them.

Why am I telling you this story? One reason: We never really "get over" the bad memories. The only way to survive our

PTSD is to override all our negative memories and emotions with positive experiences, doing something we love every day. The thing that worked best for me was to use the motivation of doing what was meaningful to me to get on with my one and only life. I cannot tell you how important this was for me.

The benefit of my traumatic stress is that it made me face the reality of my mortality. It made me realize how precious every day of life is. I urge you: take the time to ask yourself what it is that makes your life worthwhile, what it is you absolutely love to do. When you get that answer, doing that is your goal. It may take courage. It may be risky. You might have to pursue a long course in order to achieve it. You absolutely must believe in yourself, that you can do it if you put your energy and mind behind it. And it may take a lot of work. But small attainable goals will get you there, one step at a time.

My road to becoming a teacher was not straightforward, even though I had a degree in Education and had completed my student teaching many years earlier in Miami. In order to teach at the college level, I needed to get a Masters degree. While I carried a full-time schedule, I worked two twenty-hour jobs, and taught two classes at San Diego State University. Then, I had to get a PhD in order to continue teaching at SDSU, which meant driving back and forth from San Diego to the University of Southern California in the Los Angeles area every Monday, Wednesday and Friday, while still teaching classes at San Diego State. All this, just so I wouldn't have too much stress in my life!

But seriously, I didn't care how much work I had to do to achieve my goal, because teaching gave my life purpose and meaning and direction. What is more rewarding than doing something you love, something continually intriguing, exercising your brain with new ideas, always learning something new? What can give you more energy and more sense of purpose than doing what you love for the people who love you?

Finding a way you can use your unique gifts to give back to the world is one of the best ways I know to get your life back on track.

"No matter how thin you slice it,

There are always two sides."

Chapter Seven
Looking Through Another's Eyes

For twenty years I hung onto the bitterness and hatred that accompanied my story. I had been treated brutally and inhumanely for no reason. I had been grievously wronged. I harbored a feeling of hatred in my heart toward the Japanese. What they had done to me was one thing, but what they had done to my buddies was even more horrible. Whenever I got angry, I placed the blame on the Japanese. When things didn't work out for me, it was the fault of the Japanese.

The problem with this attitude is that hatred and bitterness is a poison to one's soul. I was still angry, hateful and bitter. I had reason to be so, but it was poison just the same. I wanted to let go of these poisons, but I did not know how.

Then suddenly, right on cue, life handed me an unlikely opportunity that helped me do just that.

Opening Up My Mind

One day in 1968, everything changed. That was the day I met Toru Tasaka-san, and my attitude did an "about face."

My stepson Ed was working for the International Society for Business placing foreign exchange students in summer work programs. One day, he came home from school and said, "I have a young foreign exchange student whose arrangements for living this summer are in jeopardy. The American family who was supposed to host him changed their minds. I should be able to make other arrangements by Monday, but until then, he needs a place to stay. Could he please just spend the weekend with us?"

"Of course," I said.

"There's just one thing," Ed added. "He's Japanese."

Without hesitation, I answered, "He can stay with us for the weekend. I can put up with anything for a weekend, so don't worry about it. Just bring him over."

Toru Tasaka stepped into my home that afternoon. He was young, only twenty-one years old. He had a fine, well-tuned body, with not an ounce of unwanted fat, of medium height, and with a bright smile on his face. He greeted me, and I returned his greeting in Japanese. He looked at me, and asked, "Where did you learn to speak Japanese?"

Toru could tell just from my Japanese dialect that I had learned from the less educated, rural people of his country. He was right. I had learned it from the rural workers in the coal mine at Mitsui, and from the soldiers in the field.

Then I briefly told him of my history with the Japanese.

He said, "Oh, my goodness, I don't think I'll sleep good tonight!"

We both laughed.

This was the beginning of our long and beautiful friendship. That first night, Toru sat on the floor in front of my chair, and we just started talking about everything. We talked about his work and what he planned as a career for himself. He was interested in everything. We talked about politics, my work in finance, the Germans, and the differences in culture between

America and Japan. I realized that evening that this young man of twenty-one was nothing like the other young Japanese men I had known twenty-five years before. All it took for me to realize I didn't hate all the Japanese was to meet one like Toru. Something significant was about to happen to me, without my even knowing it.

After the first weekend Toru spent with us, we agreed he should stay in our home longer; I liked how my mind was opening up, just talking with him. He wound up staying not just a weekend, but ninety-five days. Toru spent every spare moment at my side, listening to what I had to say, and sharing his knowledge of the Japanese culture with me which interested me very much.

The Way of the Warrior

I became more aware from our discussions that the Japanese society of World War II was still feudal. They were a theocracy, and worshiped their emperor Hirohito as a god. Their Shinto religion was a martial religion. They taught that other races were inferior, and that the Japanese were invincible.

Even today, there are still 110,000 national Shinto shrines in Japan. Every home had a shrine, and every family of those days genuflected toward the Imperial Palace. They gave their emperor absolute power, and had absolute loyalty to him. One hundred and twenty-three generations of Japanese had believed this.

Toru explained that the Japanese soldiers of World War II were Samurai warriors who honored the Bushido Code of conduct followed in Japan for centuries. During WWII, all the soldiers were dutiful followers of this strict code. It demanded loyalty, devotion, obedience, duty, and respect. The Bushido code helped a warrior overcome his fear of death, giving him the peace of mind and power to serve his master faithfully, even to the death, if necessary.

When I described what happened to us soldiers on the Death March, Toru was shocked. He had never been taught anything about the events of World War II, let alone the Bataan Death March. But it was his reaction to our barbaric treatment that surprised me even more, and opened my eyes to what might be the reason behind those sad events. He explained that the young soldiers on Bataan came from small villages from across the plains of Japan. There was no middle class. Half the people toiled on farms, and these 35 million people were peasant sharecroppers, paying rent to absentee landlords. They had no civil rights or liberties. Most had never seen or heard of a Caucasian, and never knew that anyone spoke a language other than Japanese. They did not know any other culture than their own. According to their beliefs and customs, we American and Filipino soldiers on Bataan were ignorant, uncaring people who didn't speak their language, and were cowards who should have killed ourselves rather than surrender. To a Samurai warrior, Toru explained, surrender was a loss of honor that also put one's entire family's honor in jeopardy. However, a Samurai warrior could regain his honor by performing seppuku, or ritual suicide. As I thought about all this, it came to me that the inhumane treatment dished out to the Americans was the same treatment they expected for themselves. In fact, in Camp 17, I witnessed a Japanese sergeant slap his subordinate Japanese private across the face with a wooden shoe. To these young men, our death would be a more honorable alternative than our surrender.

So, when an officer ordered, "Kill the prisoners if they do not obey you," those instructions absolutely had to be obeyed at all costs. They acted the way they did because they were trained that way. It made little difference whether they liked us or not. Prisoners of war were viewed as cowards, beneath contempt. They had no respect for us.

Learning all this new information began opening up my mind. I'm not saying that understanding why they acted this way was enough for me to forgive what they had done. But it did make me think. I realized what they had done was not personal to me.

It Goes Both Ways

The need for understanding went both ways. Toru had no prejudices about Americans, but we were surprised to learn he, too, had some misinformation about another group of people. When Toru came home from work that first week, he proudly showed us his first paycheck for a week's wages. Betty said, "Toru, you're our guest while you're in the United States. You should take your check and put it in the bank so you can repay your mother the money she paid to send you here from Japan."

He said, "I can't put the check in the bank. "

"Why not?" I asked.

He said, "The banks are all owned by Jews. My professor told me Jews are not trustworthy. Therefore, I certainly should not put my money in a bank."

We were surprised. "Have you ever met a Jew?" I asked.

"No," he said.

I asked him, "Toru, am I Jewish? How about Betty, or her sons Don or Ed? Are they Jewish?"

He looked at them, and then said, "No, they don't look Jewish. And you look Italian."

"Toru," I said, "we are all Jews."

He was silent a moment.

"Oh, my goodness," he said. "How will I tell my mother I stayed in a home of a former prisoner of the Japanese whose family are all Jews?"

We all had another good laugh. I said to Toru, "Hating people for no reason other than the color of their skin or for their religion is what makes war."

Inside me, an understanding was dawning. Did I have a right to hate all Japanese people because of the way some

Japanese treated me? That is what I had been doing all these years. Getting to know Toru so intimately as an individual made me realize every culture and every race had its good and bad people. How had I allowed myself to become a victim of this kind of hatred for so many years? I was no better than the people who hated Jews in the 1930s just because they were Jewish. Even in my own country of America, there was anti-Semitism. Hadn't there been a "quota" for Jews that discouraged me from even trying to get into college? My hating all the Japanese was the same thing, and now I refused to fall into that trap.

And yet, hadn't there been individual Japanese people who had been kind to me during the war years? I thought back to remember. Yes, there had. I reached back more than twenty years, and their stories unfolded before me.

The Kindness of Strangers

On the second day of the Bataan Death March, we were allowed to stop briefly so our captors could rest. I remember watching a Japanese soldier eating rice and fish from his Bento box. All us captives hadn't eaten in two days, and we were hungry, tired beyond exhaustion, and completely demoralized. The soldier turned in my direction and saw me watching him. I must have looked pitiful. Looking me in the eye, he pushed his Bento box with two spoonfuls of rice left toward me, and I took it, without a moment's hesitation. Using a piece of tree bark from the side of the road, I scooped out just enough for a good taste. Then I turned to my buddy Bob Martin, and seeing the look on his face, gave him the rest. For that brief moment of time, we were just three hungry human beings on the side of the road. That moment was forever etched in my mind.

A second memory came back to me. It was at the end of the march, when we arrived at the first prison camp, O'Donnell, half-starved from not having any food or water for four days, barely able to walk, and sick with malaria and dysentery. They crammed us into rat-infested thatched huts. One of these was designated the hospital ward, the "Zero" ward, meaning there was no place left to go. The "Z" ward was full of men who were too sick to stand, and the stench of their feces and vomit sickened all of us around it. Worse was the knowledge that these men had no hope of recovery. They were the living dead. We buried them day after day after day.

I remember sitting there, devastated, knowing the men nearby were dying, maybe in the next five or ten minutes. My life had come to this. I took out my picture of Laura from my shirt pocket, trying to come up with a reason why I should go on living. A Japanese soldier was standing nearby, eating rice from his Bento box. He saw me looking at my picture of Laura. Handing me his Bento box, he took the picture of Laura and looked at it. He smiled, and then handed it back to me. Going into his own pocket, he took out a picture of his girl, and showed it to me, as if to say, "This is my girl." I can't explain it, but all of a sudden there was this connection, this kindness shown to me by another human being at a time when I had all but given up, ready to die, not knowing what would happen to me the next minute. That one special moment made all the difference in the world to me. It gave me hope. It made me say to myself, "I've got to live."

Then there was the Japanese civilian I met while working in the Mitsui coal mine. We prisoners were divided into groups of eight or ten, with two Japanese overseers in each group. Sato Kibi-san was one of those civilians working down in the mine training us. Sato-san loved flowers and plants, and dreamed of becoming a horticulturist one day at the Golden Gate State Park in San Francisco. That was his big dream. He was about thirty-five years old, five foot-six, 140 pounds, and all muscle. Unlike most of the Japanese men I had encountered, he was polite to everyone, including us Prisoners of War.

One day he asked me if I knew anything about flowers, and right away I sensed this might be an opportunity to get us out of some work. He explained his dream of becoming a horticulturist in America, and asked if I would help him learn the English names for plants and flowers. "Of course, I'll help," I said. "Bring some pictures down into the mine, and I'll tell you their names."

At lunch break for the next four weeks, he came over to me and showed me a magazine filled with pictures of flowers, trees and shrubs. You must remember I was a city boy from Chicago. I only knew the names of cut flowers arranged in vases. Except for roses, I knew nothing. What the hell was I going to tell him? That first day, I told him the names of the few flowers I recognized, and then named all the colors and their shades. Later, back in the barracks, I asked my friends for the names of more, as many flowers as they could remember, to add to my list. All this, just so my group could sit at lunchtime and rest while I talked about flowers with Sato-san during lunch break! With his approval, my buddies would sit down in a corner of the tunnel, take off their headlamps, and close their eyes, not making a sound.

Then, on one occasion when I was in sick call, Sato-san asked a friend of mine if he would take me a gift. The next day, Sato-san smuggled a can of sweetened condensed milk into the mine for my friend to give me. This was a considerable feat at great risk to him. To smuggle it down, he had to tie the can around the inside of one of his thighs with dynamite cord. It was so hot down in the mines, we were stripped down to loincloths. That's all we wore. He had to be extremely careful no one saw it under his loincloth. Had he been caught, he would have been killed instantly, no questions asked. What a magnificent treat that can of condensed milk was! My friends all gathered around to savor its contents. I was stunned at what a friend this man was to me, to take such a great risk to smuggle a gift for me. Even with my very limited Japanese, when I got that can of milk, I understood that the Japanese civilians didn't want war just as we didn't; they wanted peace, were not angry with us, and they, too, suffered greatly from the ravages and deprivations this war had caused.

When I returned to work, I thanked him and said I regretted I could not bring him a gift in return. He said he understood, and that all he wanted was for me to stay healthy until I returned home.

We continued with his "education" for about four weeks. Each day he would bring something into the mine for each of us in the group – candy, a can of fish, a pack of cigarettes. He just wanted to show his appreciation for the time I was willing to spend with him, and his sorrow for what we had to go through.

What a wonderful man he was. I wonder if he ever made it to Golden Gate Park.

Toru's Legacy

Toru became part of the family, as close to us as a son could be, and I became as close to him as his father, who had died many years before in Nagasaki after the war. We became his Mama-san and Papa-san. When he left for home at the end of the summer, all of us cried. We wrote each other regularly over the years, and he invited us to Japan for his traditional Shinto wedding. What an experience! We were the only Caucasian people there. We met his Mama and all their Japanese friends. They were wonderful, gracious people. After the wedding, to our surprise, he and his bride invited us to go along with them to all the places his young friends went. We went to nightclubs, drinking, singing Karaoke, doing the things young people do, the only Americans among them. How warmly we were treated, just because we were friends of Toru's. That was all they needed to know.

Because of Toru, I remembered the positive aspects of his people: their work ethic, their dignity, their discipline, and their love of beauty. Most important, his explanations of the Bushido code and the Samurai warrior's beliefs, along with their feudal culture, explained so much about why and how we American POWs had been treated. The Japanese soldiers could not disobey their superiors, even if they had wanted to, or they would have suffered the same treatment we had. For the first time, I understood this brutality was not personal to me; I had not "deserved" it. It was the way of their warriors.

More than anything, this new perspective and understanding gave me the means over the following years to reach out to other Japanese people in friendship, and to let go of my bitterness, anger and hatred. It paved the way for my future friendships with Kinue, Yuka, and Ambassador Fujisaki, friendships that became so meaningful and fulfilling over the years, and made my life so much richer. These friendships were only possible because Toru Tasaka-san came to stay with us for a weekend.

What Does This Mean to You?

I know each of you reading this book has your own story, and probably that story gives you the justification to feel anger, bitterness and possibly even hatred.

But I must ask you, and you must ask yourself: how are these emotions poisoning your life? How do they hold you back? If suddenly you understood that none of it happened to you because you "deserved" it, that it was not personal to you, would that release you from those negative feelings? How would it feel, to suddenly be relieved of their burden?

Gaining understanding gave me that perspective. The brutality, the surrender, the suffering was random. This poison I was feeding, encouraging and rationalizing in my life just wasn't doing a single thing to benefit me. It was killing my soul. I just had to let it go.

Young Japanese friend, Tasaka-san with his wife, Sumiko

"Success should be measured

not just by the position you've reached,

but by the obstacles you've had to

overcome."

Chapter Eight
The Dignity of Self-Respect

For most of us who have weathered severe trauma, survivor guilt is common, and for me, overcoming it was very difficult. At the core of these feelings were self-judgment, shame and fear. I truly felt I was no good, was afraid to act for fear of reprisal, and was extremely conflicted about surviving when so many of my fellow soldiers had not.

On the positive side, my life had settled down over the years. I had found a real partner in my wife Betty, and a level of fulfillment in providing for my new family. I had finally found an occupation that challenged me and used the best of my skills and abilities to help others. To some extent, these changes began restoring my dignity and self-respect that had been so damaged during the war. I say "began," because overcoming the shame, fear, and survivor guilt took a long time to conquer.

Shame and Guilt

The reason it took me so long to overcome these feelings was due to how completely demoralized we were as POWs and slaves of the Japanese. The daily anxiety of never knowing when the war – or our lives -- would end forced us to live one day at a time. Every day we suffered the consequences of our surrender: constant humiliation. Every day we were beaten, dehumanized and abused.

To today's Americans, our captors' words, "You cowards are lower than dogs," may not explain such harsh treatment. After all, we Americans regard dogs as "man's best friend," and fuss over their care, spending big bucks on vitamins, veterinarians, and fortified dog food. But to the Japanese (and many other Asian countries), "dogs" were edible livestock, the same as cattle, pigs, goats, sheep, caribous, horses, rabbits, snakes and reptiles. To them, we were animals, and we were treated as such. Marching in the Death March, they refused to let us stop to relieve ourselves, so we had to defecate in our pants. After we arrived at prison camp O'Donnell, we were stripped of all personal items. Watches, rings, and some photographs – they plundered whatever they fancied. The dying men lay in their feces, and the stink was indescribable. The unsanitary conditions created an environment that promoted diseases. Dysentery killed more POWs than bullets. Our clothing was filthy, and bathing was rare. In Camp 17 in Japan, where we worked in the mines, the prisoners slept on thin straw mattresses, covered with one small blanket. In each poorly-constructed, unheated huts, eight men huddled together for the warmth of our combined body heat in the bitter winter cold. Our "latrine" was nothing more than holes in the floor. Men who disobeyed orders were slaughtered like pigs. On the Bataan Death March, their bodies were left to rot on the road, run over by trucks, like road kill.

Over many years of being treated as animals, we gradually came to accept their perception of ourselves. Some may call it "brainwashing." All I know is that in the process of living and working as slaves, always under the watchful eyes of someone who believed we were not worthy of living, our dignity and self-respect slowly disappeared. We came to believe deep inside ourselves that we really were failures, not much good for anyone or anything.

For me, the most difficult, most painful memories are still those where I was forced to watch my buddies tortured to death, while I was absolutely unable to prevent their suffering. Losing a buddy I lived with, ate and drank with, and joked with was like losing a member of my own family. Our respect for and commitment to each other was total. I saw our Japanese captors decapitate my friends or bury them alive, powerless to respond in any way to protect them; to respond in any way would have instantly meant my own death. Either way, my buddies had no one to protect or fight for them. That was what was so de-moralizing. My sense of morality made me want to save them, yet my own desire for survival required I hold back. I have lived these many years asking myself the same question, over and over: How could I have left them there to die, right in front of me?

Many of our men died of pure starvation or from a debilitating illness. You could tell when a man had just given up. You would know he had decided to die when he traded away his ball of rice for one last cigarette. At that first prison camp, O'Donnell, I saw it over and over again. Yet I never was able to prevent it. Even now I ask myself, "Could I have stopped it?" I don't know, but the question has haunted me all these years.

There was also no chance to grieve, remember or pay our last respects. Our lives were always on the line while our feelings were on hold, suspended in time. We had to keep focused on the immediate task at hand. Our responsibility was always to the success of the overall mission. Every time I started to think about how bad I felt, I realized I had lost another piece of my self-respect by not trying to save someone.

Where was God?

"It should have been me."

"How could I have prevented this happening to one of my friends?"

"Why, God, why me? Why did I survive?"

I went over and over what had happened, trying to make sense out of it, to know whether I had been the cause, or whether I could have done anything differently. I reassured myself that I was never the one to offer a cigarette for the ball of rice. And yet, I had survived so many unusual situations over those years, so many skirmishes with the enemy, so many misses and near misses, all while my friends perished through no fault of their own. It was, and has been, an endless cycle of self-blame and questioning.

It's strange, but through everything, I never lost my faith in God. I never blamed God for what happened. Wrestling with these questions over a long period of time, I finally concluded that some things just happen. We can't control everything. Our human minds search for a reason, a cause and effect, for a meaning to it all. But the reality of life is many random things happen which we have little or no control over.

At some point, I realized there was nothing else I could have done. Maybe there was no sense to it, I thought. What I saw happen to my buddies was not my responsibility and not my fault. I didn't do those horrible things. I was a witness to them happening. I found I could live with that. I couldn't change the past, but I could still be a living witness to the historical truth of what happened to us. By my surviving, the world would know what happened to us prisoners on Bataan. In writing down my experiences in *My Hitch In Hell*, I not only told the world about it, but I was able to take all those feelings off "hold." I think that may have been just as important.

Finding that meaning in my suffering gave me back my self-respect and my sense of control. In my life, I have found that we cannot adjust the wind, but we can always adjust the sails.

"Why me?" became "Why not me?" and I finally forgave myself for the crime of surviving when so many others had not.

Reaching Out to Others

One of the most helpful steps in recovering my sense of dignity and self-esteem was giving to others. Supporting my family and having a career was important, but I have found it's even more important to give something to others every day — money, an idea, or even a little bit of myself. I've found it was not how many goals I reached, but how many lives I touched while reaching those goals that made my life worthwhile. Giving back to others was the key to restoring my dignity and self-respect.

I can think of one particular example that illustrates how this worked in my life. As I read the daily paper, I noticed how my war trauma gave me a heightened sensitivity to soldiers in combat. I realized how much I had in common with the troops fighting overseas in Afghanistan and Iraq. I could understand how isolated they might feel, away from their families, facing an enemy, having to fire a gun, to kill after being raised "Thou shalt not kill." I wanted to do something to let those soldiers know there were people at home who appreciated what they were doing, to make them feel better. But what?

One of my strongest memories from my own war years was not getting any support from home, aside from a few letters from relatives. How I longed for even a Red Cross box, with toothpaste, cigarettes, a Hershey Bar – but of course, as a prisoner, I never got one. Because of this, I knew what it would mean just to get a package with some beef jerky, or a new pair of boot socks, or maybe a package of coffee – anything to let our warriors know someone at home cared.

So I approached some of my friends at the retirement community where we live, La Costa Glen, in Carlsbad, California. They thought the idea of sending packages to the troops was great, and said they wanted to be included in this program. About ten residents formed a non-profit company called "Care Packages From Home." One of our community members volunteered to do the legal work to make it a 501(c)3 federally approved non-profit so that donations for the troops would be tax deductible within the IRS guidelines. Within the first week we had collected about $15,000 to buy items to send to the troops. We were in business!

To get the names of overseas soldiers, we went to a website called www.anysoldier.com run by Marty Horn, a former marine. He contacts soldiers fighting overseas and instructs them to fill out forms with their names, addresses, what unit they're with, how many are in their group, and what they'd like to have. These responses are updated on the website every day. That was how we got all the necessary information for what to send to whom and where to ship it.

The administration at La Costa Glen gave us two garages for storing inventory, packing and shipping. We put up shelves, bought tables and empty boxes, and started to shop for items that the soldiers requested, which became our basic inventory. We filled up the boxes with not only their requests, but also little extras we knew they'd want, like sunglasses, lip balm, dried fruit, trail mix, nail clippers, and hygiene items for the female soldiers fighting alongside the men overseas. Our inventory wound up including 101 different items.

The residents, their friends and family, and the local community supported us in our efforts. Over the past seven years, we've collected over $750,000 and shipped over 18,000 boxes. With each box contributing to between six and ten soldiers, we calculate serving over 150,000 of our troops overseas with our care packages.

I mention this project to show how giving back can work wonders for both the giver and the recipient.

Over the years, we've received thousands of letters, and two threads go through all of them. The kids all say, "I can't believe we're getting gifts from total strangers." Secondly they say, "You have no idea what a great morale booster those boxes are. We thank you so much." What a wonderful feeling it is, knowing that we've been able to help in a little way.

American Defenders of Bataan and Corregidor

Probably the most meaningful way I was privileged to give back was to my buddies who were there in Bataan and prison camp with me, and to their families. As soon as I got home, an organization was formed called "American Defenders of Bataan and Corregidor," (ADBC).

Visiting with the family members and friends of my buddies who died was helpful to all of us. The two men who saved my life on the Bataan Death March, Bronge and Cigoi, never returned. They both died of dysentery in the camps in 1942. When I first came home, the ADBC put on a big party for us, and the mothers of Bronge and Cigoi both came up to greet me. When they said, "We're so happy to see you alive," I broke down in tears. "They're thanking me," I thought, "happy to see me, but their own sons who saved my life never came home." And yet, it helped all of us to be together, for their mothers to learn what really happened to their sons, to know what a good friends they were to me, how they heroically saved my life. To be able to cry together, and express our pain helped all of us in some way to deal with our loss.

Those first couple of years home, I visited a lot of the families from my own Tank Company B. Maintaining contact with them gave me a lifeline of support because we could discuss what we had experienced together. We understood each other on the deepest level. Over the years, I sustained a lifelong connection with several wonderful friends I will never forget.

We kept the ADBC going for over seventy years. I was aware of my fellow soldiers' ongoing needs and their progress healing from the effects of our imprisonment and slavery. I'm proud to say I was the ADBC's last National Commander. It was a sad day when we had to disband because the number of surviving POWs who were willing and able to attend a convention had dwindled to under twenty men.

Over the years, the one thing I heard over and over again from these men was how much an apology for the inhumane treatment we had endured from the companies who had enslaved us would mean. They could never return to us our health, the years we had lost in trying to recover from our emotional and physical wounds, but at least they could apologize for what they had done. It would prove to the world that our stories were not imagined, but history. Looking back, it remains a matter of deep satisfaction for me that in 1999, I was finally able to initiate a lawsuit in a bid for that apology and for justice for all of us after many years of struggling with those physical and emotional disabilities we suffered. This was one of the most meaningful pursuits of my life, and one of the most difficult, trying to make right how very much we had been wronged.

The Gift of Our Experiences

My friend, there's no other way to get past our trauma then to use it for good. Give back to the world in a positive way. With your new perspective and appreciation for the value and dignity of human life, you will find that making right the things that were wrong, performing acts of kindness and compassion, is the surest road to recovering your dignity and self-respect.

Whatever trauma you've experienced, it's given you a unique perspective, a compassion for others who've gone through the same thing. Who knows how they feel more than you? People who haven't experienced it don't understand. Work in a shelter. Volunteer your time on a suicide hot-line. Work to change the laws. By giving back, you restore a balance in the world. As much as you've suffered, you have the capacity to turn that suffering into goodness.

It's a wonderful feeling to be able to do something to help others. Believe me when I say that after all is said and done, it's not how much you accomplish in life that really counts, but how much you give to others.

*Tenney and his close friends of Company B, 192ⁿᵈ Tank Battalion.
Upon returning home, Tenney received a lifetime of support
from the families of his deceased buddies.*

Chapter Nine
The Cry for Justice

When something terribly unfair happens and turns your life upside-down, after the damage has been done, after you've picked up the pieces, you may hope beyond hope that someday, in some small way, justice will be served. I know I certainly did. That was why I seized the opportunity to pursue justice when it became possible fifty-three years after the war was over. It seemed like the culmination of a lifetime of effort to hold accountable those who had wronged us.

If justice could be served, what outcome would you want from a court of law? What compensation would be reasonable enough to satisfy you? Seriously think about this. If you have dreams of righting your wrongs through the courts of justice, you have to consider how that dream might be unrealistic. What are the true chances of getting your preferred outcome? You must factor these into the equation before you decide to take the risk of putting your pain on public display in a court of law.

In my case, I was brought up with the expectation that criminal behavior would be punished. "An eye for an eye..." and all that. "Do unto others as you would have others do unto you" was a given. In America, we pride ourselves on having a just system of law balanced with fairness and mercy. That's what makes our nation great, I thought.

But we're not talking about some heavenly tribunal of angels meting out judgments. Our human justice system is still evolving, an imperfect idea rendered by imperfect people. It depends on the integrity, impartiality and fairness of our courts...and often, they do not exhibit these qualities. I just want to emphasize this so you are aware of the risk. If you're putting your hopes for recovery on the American justice system, and it fails, then what? Be very clear about what you need to get from this experience before you get into it. You might have to modify your expectations.

My pursuit of justice took over seventy years to unfold, and at no time was any of it easy to accomplish. However, because I was very clear about what outcome I hoped to achieve, my story does have a happy ending.

Post-War Justice

In our case, we wanted an apology from the corporations that used and abused us, who subjected us to endless torture and enriched their own fortunes on the backs of our slave labor.

As American soldiers, we accepted the risks of war. We knew we might be captured or die, and we were willing to die with honor. But our honor was completely disregarded by the Japanese in their conquest of the Philippines. What we never anticipated was being placed into servitude for private industrial giants of Japan to further the enemy's war effort. No warrior expects to be made a slave of a conquering army…not in the twentieth century, and certainly not in the twenty-first.

After we were captured, the prisoners were sold to at least forty-four Japanese private business conglomerates (the *zaibatsu*) to labor without compensation. These companies' "miraculous" financial recoveries had their origin in the gift of our free labor. Some of these companies became multi-billion dollar industries, including Kawasaki, Mitsubishi, Nippon, and Showa Denko, and Mitsui, owner of the mine where I labored for almost three years. Today, Mitsui is the third largest corporation in the world.

I first contacted our State Department about compensation from Mitsui for my labor when I returned from the war in 1946. I asked about POWs making claims against the Japanese companies who had enslaved us, and representatives from our government responded immediately. "Don't do anything personally," they said. "You don't need to hire a lawyer." They were aware of what had happened, they said, and were taking care of it. They'd get back to me. Interesting that in all these years, I haven't heard from anyone. I'm still waiting for someone to get back to me.

True, some Japanese war criminals were held accountable for their crimes, and were punished, but it was only a fraction of those responsible. After the Japanese surrendered, a United States Military tribunal convicted General Homma of the Imperial Japanese Army of being responsible for the troops carrying out the invasion of the Philippines and the Bataan

Death March. They executed him by firing squad on April 3, 1946.

5,700 Japanese nationals were also initially indicted for Class B crimes against humanity, most of which were for prisoner abuse. They were accused of plundering our private property, forcing us to labor under inhumane conditions, maiming, torturing, and murdering us. However, at the Tokyo War Crimes Trials, of 750 accused of these crimes, only twenty-eight were prosecuted. Seven were executed, including General Tojo. Sixteen were given life in prison. When the American occupation of Japan ended in 1952, most Japanese serving sentences in Tokyo's Sugamo Prison were freed. In 1954, our own U.S. Secretary of State, John Foster Dulles, changed the period required for eligibility for parole to ten years. By 1958, all the rest of the prisoners had been released.

Regarding Japan's bacteriological and chemical warfare experiments at Unit 731 on live human subjects (many of whom were civilians), those who were responsible for the experiments were never brought to trial. The American Supreme Commander of the Allied Powers, General MacArthur, gave immunity to them in exchange for their data on germ warfare in 1948.

Most disappointing to us POWs was the War Crimes Trial prosecutors' decision in 1946 to drop indictments against all the heads of the major Japanese companies who had enslaved us. Those who were most responsible for our enduring suffering were exonerated, never brought to trial.

How many Americans know anything about this? Only a fraction of the Japanese war criminals of World War II were punished in any manner. Of those who were punished, many were released early by our own U.S. Secretary of State, and the companies who enslaved us were exempted from any punishment at all. You can understand now why I say human justice is imperfect! And that was only the beginning.

The 1951 Peace Treaty

Considered from our country's point of view, 1951 was filled with the anxiety of the Cold War. China had a Communist regime, the Soviets threatened worldwide expansion, the Korean War was raging, and Japan was caught right in the middle. More than anything, the United States needed a stable Japan, and so General MacArthur was assigned the task of establishing a strong democracy and economy there. In addition, to help Japan rebuild, the United States gave them $2 billion in economic aid.

Then in 1951, John Foster Dulles, Secretary of State to President Eisenhower, drafted a post-war peace treaty between the United States and Japan. Unfortunately for us former prisoners of war, this treaty prohibited any slave-labor lawsuits for reparations or compensation beyond what they stipulated. The treaty called for Japan to transfer all its assets in Allied or neutral countries to the International Red Cross to be distributed to national agencies to compensate the POWs and their families. But the United States waived its claim to the Red Cross funds…the only Allied nation to do so. "We'll take care of our own," said the U.S. State Department.

Here's how they took care of us: Under the "War Claims Acts of 1948 and 1952, they gave us $1 a day for missed meals, and $1.50 for each day we labored or were subjected to inhumane treatment. Most POWs of the Japanese who were subjected to forced labor received an average of $2600. That's it. But what we wanted was an apology, some acknowledgment of the inhumane treatment we had endured, and how we had been denied the food that would have sustained us to perform that strenuous labor.

Our one hope in the Peace Treaty was Article 26, the "Most Favored Nation" clause. It stated, "Should Japan make a peace settlement or war claims settlement with any state granting that state greater advantage than those provided by the present treaty, those same advantages shall be extended to the United States." That seemed fair. Perhaps that provision would allow us to finally get our due.

The Years Pass

Only much later, when we were able to finally contract with a law firm to file a class-action lawsuit, did we learn from their research that the British, Australian, New Zealand and Dutch governments had passed legislation to compensate each of their soldiers who had been forced into slave labor with $25,000 apiece. The German government acknowledged their wrongdoing, and established a fund to provide monetary benefits to their victims. Even our own country gave compensation to every Japanese-American who had been uprooted from their homes and businesses and interned in camps in the United States. The $1.25 billion Civil Liberties Act in 1988, awarded $20,000 to each internee, and President Ronald Reagan delivered a formal apology on behalf of the American people to all of them. By contrast, Japan not only provided no compensation to any of us, but would not even acknowledge that they had done anything wrong.

Why couldn't we get the same treatment, the same apology from the Japanese? And why couldn't our own country accord us the same payment, the same dignity they extended to the Japanese-Americans? The Allies helped rebuild Japan, Germany and Italy, but nobody helped us rebuild our lives. We had to do that all on our own.

The Tide Turns

One of my neighbors, after reading my book *My Hitch In Hell*, suggested I file a lawsuit against Mitsui, but the Statute of Limitations had already expired. Then, in 1999, the State of

California passed Senate Bill 1245 extending the limitation to the end of 2010 for "all victims of WWII slave labor abuses to collect damages from German companies *or their allies* that profited from their labor." The only stipulation was the company named for damages had to be conducting business in California.

A local San Diego law firm became interested in our search for justice. Dave Casey, Jr. and two others from his firm came to my home to discuss it. After hearing my story, and seeing that I had written evidence – a document written by my doctor in Japan stating I had been beaten with a pickax and hammer in Omuta, Japan – they were excited to pursue it. They were gathering together a group of prominent attorneys in San Francisco who wanted to take on a social justice case of national interest, and asked if I would be willing to talk to this group. Everything was arranged for me: ticket, hotel, limousine – all paid for. I told my story again to a roomful of lawyers, a mega-firm of specialists. They were from everywhere in the United States: Washington, D.C., Atlanta, San Diego, Palm Desert, New Orleans, and Jackson, Mississippi. These were some of the most sought-after professionals in the industry. Their collective expertise encompassed researchers, treaty experts, litigators, strategists…everything necessary for a national case, including deep pockets to finance it. It didn't take much time for them to make a decision. After lunch, they announced they wanted to take this case on as their social issue. We signed a contract, and they agreed to represent our cause for no fee.

It was so gratifying to be supported by such highly intelligent and accomplished people. They were enthusiastic about the strength of our case, and outraged by the cruelty we had endured. I can't overestimate the value of that support. Finally to feel understood, to have intelligent, articulate people on our side for once, was of true benefit to those of us suffering from PTSD. Some of our POWs had never before been able to fully tell their story. Just the power of someone listening to our testimonies and recognizing what we had endured was so important. It is one value you will get from going to a court of law.

The Emotional Cost of Our Suffering

I had previously calculated the financial value of our labor for a fellow POW Robert Aldrich when he filed his own lawsuit in 1987 in New Mexico. Unfortunately, he never lived to see his day in court. In 1988, he died very suddenly.

Over the years, so many of us had already died. Of the 27,465 Americans captured and interned by the Japanese, only about 16,000 returned home. In 1999, the year our trial began, only a third of those, or 5,695 American slave laborers, were still alive. Today, in the year 2014, less than one hundred are left, and those of us who made the Bataan Death March number under ten.

It was the emotional cost that was impossible to quantify. Additional reparations were allowed by the California Senate Bill 1245 for physical injuries and for the continued emotional distress caused by torture and beatings -- the origin of what we now call our PTSD. The American men who survived slave labor in these Japanese companies came home to a lifetime of lingering medical problems and permanent injuries caused by that labor. We were young men chronologically, but were old men in spirit when we returned from the war.

Frank Bigelow, a fellow prisoner in Omuta's Camp 17, testified at the trial how he went to work on a day in January, 1944 into that unsafe Mitsui mine, only to have part of the ceiling fall on his leg and crush it. His buddies carried him up 1,600 feet to the surface, where he lay bleeding on a stone floor for five hours till the work shift was over. The only thing that kept him from bleeding to death was that the weather was so cold his blood coagulated. Still, his lower leg had to be amputated by the camp's American doctor, Thomas Hewlett, without anesthesia. To save what remained of the leg from infection, maggots were stuffed inside the bandage to eat the dead tissue.

We suffered all kinds of health problems stemming from the conditions we endured over those years. Many of the POWs who toiled at the mines at Omuta walked permanently bent forward for the rest of their lives, after working for years in those mine tunnels less than four feet high. Our unheated and filthy barracks were crawling with fleas, lice and vermin. But the unsanitary conditions were the least of it. We were starving. Our daily diet was 80% rice and 20% filler, less than 600 calories for men sent out to work twelve-hour shifts. A normal diet for miners working those long shifts would have been at least 3000 calories. The average weight loss we incurred over the years was between 70-100 pounds. Starvation and disease were the leading causes of the 40% death rate among our men. Our clothes hung on us, and we looked like human skeletons. All of us suffered from malnutrition, which affected our health permanently. This was one source of our PTSD, the stress we lived with day after day for the rest of our lives. It was for this that we wanted an apology.

I find it ironic that Mitsui's coal mining complex at Omuta was built in 1917 by American engineers; twenty-five years later, American slaves were forced to mine that coal to support Japan's war against our own people and our Allies. They had the largest coal mine in Japan, with nine levels, yet could only burn one hour's worth of coal a day to heat our barracks during one of Japan's coldest winters on record. Explain that to the jury, please! The mine operated until 1997, when there was a big cave-in that killed about five hundred people. It had been unsafe for years.

Congressional Support

Over the course of the four years of our trial, I was called upon to testify, with several of my peers, at different hearings in Washington, D.C. before Congress. One hearing concerned the interpretation of Article 26, the "Most Favored Nation" clause of the 1951 Peace Treaty. Our law firm's researchers had discovered that the Japanese had gone beyond the 1951 treaty's provisions to compensate POWs from the countries of Denmark, Burma, the British Commonwealth, the Netherlands, and several others. They gave these other countries preferential treatment in new treaties, but refused outright to honor Article 26 of our treaty to provide those same benefits to the Americans. But our cause was undermined by the U.S. State Department, who decided that the treaty's provisions only applied to nations, not individuals.

We had tremendous support from Senator Orrin Hatch of Utah and Dianne Feinstein of California who were both on the U.S. Senate Judiciary Committee. They understood our situation, and worked diligently on our behalf, sponsoring amendments to get reparations for us. Even so, nothing seemed to be working in our favor.

Congressman Mike Honda, the son of a Japanese-American internee, was also on our side. The U.S. Civil Liberties Act of 1988 which awarded every Japanese internee $20,000 had impressed him that we POWs of the Japanese should be accorded similar dignity. He introduced House Resolution 1198, the "Justice for United States Prisoners of War Act of 2001" which called for an official apology from Japan for its inhumane wartime acts, which was passed into committee on March 22, 2001. The fact that a Japanese-American would speak up on our behalf, would go out on a limb for us to insist Japan apologize because it was the right thing to do, had great meaning for all of us. Then all the good feelings disappeared quickly. After the bill went into the committee, the chairman never took it out of committee, and the bill died.

You just can't get around it. In spite of all the work and support from Congress, politics played an important role in our court case. They aren't kidding when they say, "You can't fight City Hall."

The Trial Drags On

Nevertheless, our trial was not against Japan, but against their corporations.

The *zaibatsu* had hired plenty of American lawyers, all being paid millions of dollars, to defend them... but their primary and only witness was our very own State Department. It was the U.S. Department of State who testified against us, insisting that initial payments to us under the treaty were payment enough, and that those payments had satisfied our reparations. End of story.

August 17, 2000 was a hard day for all of us when Judge Vaughn Walker of Federal District Court delivered his statement in the Federal courthouse in San Francisco, the same courthouse where the 1951 Peace Treaty had been signed. He said, "History has vindicated the wisdom of the Treaty of Peace with Japan. And while full compensation for plaintiffs has been denied these former prisoners and countless other survivors of the war, the immeasurable bounty of life for themselves and their posterity in a free society and in a more peaceful world services the debt." In other words, being alive and living in a free society should be bounty enough for us.

The American POWs were shocked and insulted. Was he saying that because we led respectable lives today, we had no right to any apology or compensation from the Japanese? His words made us feel –all over again – that we were lower than dogs. It was as if he were saying, "You're living, aren't you? Isn't that enough? What more do you want? You're not entitled to anything more."

I mention this to you as a precaution. Thoughtless remarks from people in power can affect your level of stress, trigger reactions you thought you had long since buried. I still feel the sting of that judge's words.

Of course, our lawyers remained upbeat. "Don't take this as a defeat," they said. "We expected this outcome at the District level. Don't worry. We'll file an appeal. We're prepared to take it all the way to the Supreme Court if we need to." And there was still the "Justice for Veterans" amendment to the Department of Defense's appropriations bill pending in Congress which would give every still-living POW forced into slavery by the Japanese $10,000 apiece. So we kept our hopes high, and waited for justice to be served.

For me, the most important profit from the trial was a different form of compensation. Along the way, our cause was publicized nationwide, giving it legitimacy and building sympathy for our suffering. The media ran story after story in national magazines, including *Parade*, *People*, and *Reader's Digest*, and newspapers including the *New York Times*, the *Washington Post*, the *San Diego Union Tribune*, the *Boston Globe*, and *Asahi Shimbun*, Japan's major daily newspaper. We received TV coverage on CNN, ABC News, MSNBC, 20/20, and interviews by Peter Jennings, Barbara Walters and Dan Rather. I was asked to speak before the Veterans of Foreign Wars, Disabled American Veterans, and many other concerned civic organizations. The personal benefits of these experiences were immeasurable. In a way, the ability to finally tell our story to the people of America, and even to the people of Japan, was a form of justice being served in the court of public opinion.

Your Day in Court

Life has an inherent risk, and an underlying unfairness. Our human system of justice is riddled with risk, flaws, politics, and trauma of its own. What is the cost to you, and what are the possible benefits? You have to think carefully before you put yourself through the trauma of a trial. What humiliation will you have to go through upon cross-examination in order to tell your story? What will be the cost? What are the benefits, bottom line?

On the other hand, if all you want is the chance to tell your story before an impartial audience who will witness your truth, and if that is enough, then maybe the outcome is not so important. Then go ahead and have your day in court. May justice ultimately be served, and may your stress be relieved in so doing.

In the meantime, we waited for the Supreme Court to hear our case.

No. _____

In the

Supreme Court
of the United States

LESTER I. TENNEY, *et al.*,
Petitioners,

v.

MITSUI & CO., LTD., MITSUI & CO. (USA), INC.,
MITSUI MINING CO. LTD.,
and MITSUI MINING USA INC.,
Respondents,

On Petition for a Writ of Certiorari
to the United States Court of Appeals
for the Ninth Circuit

PETITION FOR A WRIT OF CERTIORARI

Steven M. Schneebaum*/
PATTON BOGGS LLP
2550 M Street, N.W.
Washington, D.C. 20037
(202) 457-6300
Counsel for Petitioners
*/ *Counsel of Record*

June 4, 2003

*Our plea for justice ended when the
Supreme Court refused to hear our case...*

"It's not how much you accomplish in life that really counts,

it's how many lives you've touched

in getting there."

Chapter Ten
How Can I Forgive?

And then, just like that, it was over. The Supreme Court refused to hear our lawsuit. The American Prisoners of War would not receive reparations from the private Japanese companies who had enslaved us and profited from our unpaid labor. They would offer no apology. Why should they? Our Supreme Court had just ruled in their favor. So that was that. They won; we lost.

I couldn't believe it. I had been certain our cause was so defensible that justice would be served. I should have known after being a prisoner all those years that nothing is ever certain. We had just spent four years of our lives struggling to pursue justice, all for this?

Two weeks before, Congress had passed the Department of Defense appropriations bill, but without the "Justice for Veterans" amendment that would have given every still-living POW slave laborer $10,000 in reparations. Then a few weeks later the highest court in the land turned away our appeal on the lawsuit.

I felt betrayed by my own government. They abandoned us on Bataan to fight with no food, no medical supplies, and no ammunition. They surrendered us to the Japanese, who tortured, starved, beat, and enslaved us. During all our years in captivity, we did not forsake America or what it stood for. Now America was forsaking us. We were still pawns in their game. Nothing had changed in sixty years. It felt like we were being surrendered again.

My fellow combatant Harold Poole, when asked by the media about how we Prisoners of War could recover from this loss, answered, "You come home, and forgive and forget. Just let it go. It's the only way to find peace."

I had a problem with his statement, "Just let it go."

Was it the money? No, I didn't care about the money. That debt had been on the books for years. Our State Department had said, "We'll take care of our own." Well, this was how they took care of us. We received nothing – not one red dime. Now we were all old men! Why carry that burden, that resentment around anymore, wasting all my energy chasing after it? No, money was the least of it.

Only three things mattered to me now. I wanted the Japanese people to know about this shameful chapter in their history that was not in any of their textbooks, and not in their collective memory. Second, I wanted some acknowledgment of what we had endured, a restoration of our dignity. Most of all, I wanted an apology for the inhumane treatment. Japan and their industrial giants had to take some responsibility for what they'd done. How else could I forgive?

Accepting the Past

Harold was talking about letting go. Well, I had let go of the things that were beyond my control. I understood that some things just happen randomly, period. The surrender, the march, not being able to help my fellow soldiers while they were being tortured – all those things had been beyond my control. I had accepted that what happened, happened. I couldn't change the past.

The thing was, acceptance is passive, and being a passive victim was not my way. The whole key to my survival and getting my life back was about taking control of what I could: choosing a positive attitude, choosing my thoughts, setting goals, preserving my values and restoring my dignity. Sure, you can't change the past, but you can look forward to the future and do something about it. I accept that I don't get to choose how or when I'm going to die, but I sure as hell can decide how I'm going live.

I didn't want to forget the past; I wanted to use it. I had to train my mind to not blame anybody – God or anyone else – for what happened. Then I had to look for ways to use what was wrong, and actively make it right. That's the difference between acceptance and forgiveness.

So where could I go from here? I had to do a lot of hard thinking about letting go and forgiveness.

Even When You Lose, You Win

Up to the time of the lawsuit, I didn't have a lot of experience with forgiveness. The one instance that stood out in my memory was forgiving Laura. When I returned home from the war, I discovered the woman I had married, whose picture I carried and dreamed about for all those years, was now married to another man. I knew the problem. I called her. After tearful hellos, she said, "I thought you had died over there. I am so happy to hear you're alive. I hope your health is good. Do you understand?" No one had to tell me. She thought I was dead, so why wait any longer? That's why she thought it would be all right to remarry.

As devastated as I was, I knew I had to see her. My family wanted to know why. I said, "She has to know that what she did was honorable." Laura was so young, only twenty-three, with her whole life ahead of her. She had the right to a full life. Releasing her so she could have her life back was the honorable thing for me to do.

We had eloped when Laura was visiting me in Fort Knox, Kentucky where our tank battalion was training before being sent overseas. During her visit, in one of the little cities nearby, we found a Justice of the Peace who married us. I went off to war, taking the legal papers with me. Laura was notified that I was Missing in Action and presumed dead, but though she waited for some word from our government for three long years, she received nothing. Meantime, her younger sister had fallen in love and wanted to marry. When her father told her that her younger sister couldn't marry until she did, Laura couldn't produce any evidence to convince him she already was married. The pressure on her was tremendous. Her friends advised her, "Get on with your life." Finally she began to see a man who she felt she could love, and when he proposed, she accepted — for her sister's sake as well as her own. And now, when I saw her, she was pregnant.

I realized that as hard as this was on me, what she had to do must have been just as difficult. The fact that I was alive, not dead, and that she had married someone else must have weighed on her so heavily. I loved her, so I had to let her go -- for both our benefits.

Yet, despite my broken heart, I realized that even loving, but losing, her had its positive side. My dream of being with her again, and the steadfast belief that I would return one day were what had kept me alive. For that, I would always be grateful. That was my first lesson in forgiveness, and it was a hard one.

Giving Up the Luxury of Hating

I learned about letting go of my hatred and resentment twenty years later when Toru, our Japanese exchange student, came for a weekend, and wound up staying with us for ninety-five days. Toru had no preconceptions of what life was all about. He just lived it. He did not have any hate. He didn't hate Americans. He loved every little bit of life, every minute of it. He was a young kid growing up in a good time in history, so innocent, so eager to learn everything. Being with him changed me. Betty and I cried when he had to get on a plane and go home, and he also cried like a baby. It was a sad day for all of us. We learned to love the boy; he became like a son to us. For years he called us "Mama-san and Papa-san." That's when I started to realize, "I don't hate this kid. He's Japanese, but what difference does it make?"

After knowing Toru, when I met other Japanese people, their race didn't make any difference anymore. I realized my bitterness and hatred for the Japanese "people" all those years dissolved after I had learned to love one Japanese "person." I saw that my hatred had been as destructive to my spirit as fighting had been to my body. As Nelson Mandela said upon leaving prison, "As I walked out the door toward the gate that would lead to my freedom, I knew if I didn't leave my bitterness and hatred behind, I'd still be a prisoner." I had created a narrow opening in my heart by being willing to love Toru, and that alone began to change me.

A New Perspective

I met Toru thirty-five years before the lawsuit we just lost. How could letting go of my hatred and resentment against the Japanese people help me in this situation today? I asked myself where I stood on those three things I hoped the trial would accomplish? People say, "When you don't like a thing, change it. If you can't change it, then find a way to change the way you think about it." That's what I had to do: change my thinking. Maybe I hadn't "lost." Maybe I could find other ways to capitalize on what I had gained from losing the trial, and still accomplish those goals.

Even before the lawsuit, I had been educating people about what happened in the Pacific in World War II. I published *My Hitch In Hell* in 1995, which led to an invitation to be keynote speaker at the World Conference on Peace in Japan that same year. Then in 1997, I was asked to be keynote speaker at the British cemetery in Yokahama for their annual memorial service. The cemetery has one casket with the remains of forty-five American POWs, but this was the first year an American was invited to be present among representatives from all the different countries. A retired Japanese professor, Yuka Ibuki, was at the service, looking for someone with personal experience as a POW during the war to come talk to schools in Japan about what happened to us. After hearing my speech, she emailed me an invitation to return to Japan to do so. She used her own money, an inheritance from her mother, for this project. I made five trips to Japan between 1999 and 2008, speaking to thousands of Japanese students at thirteen colleges, high schools and middle schools.

I had gained a deeper understanding through my talks with Toru of how the soldiers could have treated me as they did. I used everything Toru had explained to me about their culture, how the Japanese soldiers were from little villages, living very feudal lives. With my new perspective, I was able to approach the students with the truth about what had happened, yet without hatred. It was a profound experience, for them and for me. Those kids learned about something that was not in their textbooks.

"When you hear my talk," I began, "I don't want you to get the idea that I'm saying all Japanese were bad. That is not what I'm saying. Some people just didn't know any better. They thought what they were doing was right."

We talked about how, in a war, everyone suffers. The Japanese people, the average citizens, wanted no part of that war. It was strictly a military decision. The common people suffered with death, lack of food, and the horrible destruction of Nagasaki and Hiroshima.

Then I told them the story of my experiences.

They asked me how it was possible that people of their grandparents' generation could do these horrible things. I told them I had come to believe there were many causes.

First, miscommunication. The guards in the Imperial Japanese Army were simple country people with little education. They shouted orders at us in Japanese. They didn't realize we couldn't understand them.

"Imagine a young soldier of nineteen, trained in the Bushido code. His commanding officer says, 'These prisoners have to walk to prison camp. If they don't walk, kill them.'

"The kid sees me, an American soldier fall down, and he says to me in Japanese, 'Hey, buddy, get up. You've got to get going.' But I don't know what he's saying because I don't speak a word of Japanese.

"'Hey! Did you hear what I said? I said to get going. I don't want to kill you. I was told by my commanding officer to get you to walk or kill you,'" he screams.

"But I can't move. And I don't understand a word he's shouting at me.

"Now he's getting frustrated and yells, 'Do you hear me? Are you disobeying me on purpose? I don't want to kill you, but you're making me do it!'"

I reminded them that the ancient Samurai tradition of the Bushido warrior required complete obedience, and willingness to follow orders unquestioningly. When we didn't respond to our captors' orders, they thought we were disobeying, but we just plain didn't understand them.

Also, physical abuse was common in the Imperial Army. They considered it a tool for toughening up their soldiers for combat. Since they treated their own men badly, they didn't consider it unusual to abuse their captives.

Then there was the fact that being a guard was the worst possible position. They assigned troublemakers, alcoholics, and misfits to the job. They were shamed in the eyes of their peers, and took it out on us. Most of these guards were youngsters, eager to impress a fellow guard looking on by the horrendous things they did. They also hadn't anticipated the huge number of prisoners they would have to feed and accommodate, and certainly our deaths only made their jobs easier. Most of all, the fact that we surrendered, rather than fighting to the death as the Japanese Bushido warrior would have done, made us undeserving of respect in their eyes.

Forgiveness Does Not Condone What Happened

I emphasized to the students that all these motivations did not excuse their atrocities in any way. It was just a way to understand them, not to condone them. We talked about

178

the need to understand each other in order not to repeat the mistakes of the past, to forge true friendships based on trust and understanding, and how the acknowledgment of painful truths leads to forgiveness.

In Japan, at the universities, students do not ask their professors questions, because to ask a question is considered challenging, and students would never challenge them publicly. But after the class was over, all these kids came up to me, asking questions, and telling me what happened with their grandparents.

"He was in the war, but I don't know where he was."

"I went home and asked my grandfather about the war, but he would not talk about it."

"I can't get a word from him. He won't discuss it. We know nothing."

Forgiving Does Not Require Forgetting

After I came home, I received many emails from these students. "It was hard to believe our grandparents' generation did such terrible things," one said. "We have a dark past, and what happened can never be changed. But we must learn from our history and not repeat it. We must show the world we have changed."

"Young people today don't know about the terror of war. We had no description in our books, only about the bomb in Hiroshima. We need to know the truth. Talking to each other like you did would build a bridge to the next generation."

"Tenney-san's desire for peace has been conveyed to my heart. We should know about war and pass it on to the next generation. People who do not know about war will easily start another one."

Talking with these students changed me. For all of human history, men have waged war. Now together we spoke about waging peace.

Leave the Door of Friendship Open

What about receiving an apology for the inhumane treatment? That was harder.

When I filed the lawsuit in 1999, a woman named Kinue Tokudome, who was very interested in rebuilding the relationship between Japan and the United States, came to listen to our case. She was living here with her husband who was working in America for a Japanese company at the time. Kinue understood what we had endured as prisoners of the Japanese, and had founded a program called "the U.S. – Japan Dialogue on POWs." We became very close. She introduced me to Clay Perkins who was funding her program. When Yuka wanted to translate and publish my book in Japan, Clay and Kinue put up the money in 2003, and then Clay bought two hundred of those books for every member of the Japanese Diet to read.

I became aware in 1995 that the Japanese had invited all POWs and their families—all POWs except the Americans -- to Japan, all expenses paid. I couldn't believe it. I contacted our congressmen, our senators, and even our President asking how could this be allowed? The response I received was, "Oh, it's not that important. Let it go." Not that important? Japan spent $16 million on a trip for these other POWs, but made no formal apology to them. Between 1999 and 2008, I met with members of the Japanese Diet to explain how important it would be for their government to apologize to the American POWs for the wartime abuse. But although these efforts were widely reported in their media, the apology to us never came. Even the United

States Ambassador to Japan refused to see me or even talk with me.

Then on Veterans Day in 2008, after being invited to lay a wreath on the Tomb of the Unknown Soldier in the Arlington National Cemetery in Washington, D.C., I received a call. Would my wife Betty and I come to the official residence of Ichiro Fujisaki, the Japanese Ambassador to the United States? He had only been on the job for five months, but he knew I had not received any response from Japanese officials all those years. It was the call I had been waiting for.

Chapter Eleven
A Prisoner No More

When I met the Japanese Ambassador Ichiro Fujisaki, I was the last National Commander of the American Defenders of Bataan and Corregidor. Our veteran's organization of former POWs of the Japanese was going to be disbanded the next year in 2009 due to the advanced age and declining health of our members. I described in detail to the Ambassador the torture and enslavement we had endured.

"What do you want?' he asked me.

"We want equal treatment. We want a trip to Japan for American POWs. We want an apology from the Japanese government and the companies that enslaved us for the brutal and inhumane treatment we received, and we want to visit the prison camps with our families." I was all business. I didn't need to be buddies with the enemy. I just wanted an apology.

But I had another reason for wanting desperately to go back to Japan. Our exchange student Toru was dying of cancer, and we knew he did not have much time. I told Ambassador Fujisaki and his wife about how much our friendship with Toru meant to us, how much it had fueled my working to establish a friendship between our nations. I wanted to visit Toru's grave, if nothing else.

He said he would see what he could do.

As we left their home, the ambassador's wife ran out to our waiting car with tears in her eyes to say goodbye, and affirm they would do all they could for us. Our friendship with Toru, and our desire to pay that respect touched her very deeply.

I remember that last meeting of the American Defenders of Bataan and Corregidor. It was in May of 2009 in San Antonio, Texas. Five hundred people were there, seventy-three of them survivors of the Bataan Death March of April 1942. It was sixty-seven years later, and our members were in failing health, on their real last death march. I sat down in my hotel room and called Ambassador Fujisaki. Would he be willing to come and offer an apology to our men at their last meeting on Saturday?

"Yes," he said.

At 12:15 on May 30th, Ambassador Fujisaki delivered that official apology to us. He said he was speaking for the government of Japan as he said, "We extend a heartfelt apology for our country having caused tremendous damage and suffering to many people including prisoners of war, those who have undergone tragic experiences in the Bataan peninsula and Corregidor Island." It was the first time a Japanese official had explicitly apologized to us, and it felt good. In a letter he wrote to me five years later, Fujisaki wrote, "My visit to San Antonio was one of the best things I did during my over forty years of service in the government. With your initiative and strong will, I was able to do the right thing."

After lunch, in his hotel room, Ambassador Fujisaki told me he would do all he could to ease our stress and arrange a trip to Japan for us.

Life is What Happens While You're Busy Making Plans

In the sixty-five years that had passed since I came home from the war, I had always tried to stay busy and active. Now

I was enjoying my golden years to the fullest, but suddenly noticed a disturbing change in my energy level. I was getting tired very easily. Playing tennis was becoming a chore. I noticed I could hardly hit the ball back from a light serve. This was not like me. Even walking was starting to be a hardship, making me pant and always be out of breath. What was happening?

I went to my cardiologist, and after a brief examination, he told me my aortic valve wasn't working right. Simple aging had caused a build-up of calcium that hardened and thickened the valve, narrowing it and keeping it from opening completely, hindering the blood flow, and making the heart have to work much harder. "You need a new valve," he said, "but you are not a candidate for open heart surgery."

"What does that mean?" I asked, stunned.

"It means time is running out. If you don't replace it, you have a year or two at the most." And then he said, "But you're ninety years old. Do you want to live forever?"

What kind of question was that? And why was this happening now? In my head, that same nagging question: "Why me, God? Why me? Don't you know what I've been working on? Don't you know how close we are to achieving it?"

I had just received an early morning call from the State Department, announcing that Ambassador Fujisaki, as promised, had contacted them about a visitation program for former American POWs to Japan. Furthermore, Fujisaki told them he "would like Dr. Tenney to lead that group and make all the plans for the visit." Fifteen years of work were coming to fruition.

My mind was racing. I was already preparing what we would do. Our first stop would be at the U.S. Embassy in Japan. This would be my payback for the way they treated me all those years when I tried to get an answer to why no Americans were included or honored with a visitation program. Then we needed to meet with either the Prime Minister or the Minister of Foreign Affairs at the Japanese Diet, where an apology would be extended to the POWs under the lights of Japanese TV and the watchful eyes of the world press. That was a must. We wanted the world to know what had happened. Then we needed a day for each POW to visit the city of his choice, most likely the one where he was used as a slave laborer. After such a long hiatus, we wanted to return with our families to show them where we spent those three long years.

But first I had to survive! As plans for this long awaited visit were going through my mind, I suddenly realized I might not make it. If I couldn't get that new heart valve, I might die without fulfilling my dream of reconciliation. I turned to the cardiologist and asked, "What could be done?"

He said, "Well, we could stretch the valve a little every three or four months to relieve your symptoms."

That didn't sound very promising. There had to be something better!

Dying is Easy; It's the Living That's Hard

I have had my share of stress, but nothing like this. Everything was compounding, between wanting that apology, needing to be treated equally with all the other POWs from other countries, and knowing how positively this visit would affect all the survivors. So much was riding on this visitation program, but now there was a time bomb in my chest. The biggest stress of all was, "Would I make it?"

I've found, though, that when the chips are down in my life, the adrenalin pushes everything else aside, and the need for action takes over. I started putting my thoughts in order: I must be able to travel to Japan. That required a new heart valve. Where do I find one? Most important, was there a non-invasive procedure that could replace it without open-heart surgery? These were the questions I had to answer.

Being a young ninety-year-old, my first thought was "search the Internet." Wouldn't you know, my search for a "minimally invasive heart surgery for aortic valve replacement" revealed an experimental procedure right here in San Diego for a non-invasive method inserting "The Edwards SAPIEN Transcatheter Heart Valve." It was made of tissue from the protective sac that surrounds a cow's heart. They cut a small opening in an artery in the leg, and then pushed the tube through the blood vessels until it reached the damaged valve in the heart. Then they'd blow up the balloon on the end of the tube to expand the new valve so it would stay in place.

The valve was not yet approved by the FDA, though; it was still too experimental and new. While it was available in Europe, the valve was still in a clinical trial here in the United States.

It only could be used for patients who couldn't undergo open-heart surgery. Well, that was exactly my situation. Obviously, this was what I was seeking.

It was not without risks, however. Data from early experiences here in the United States indicated that patients who received the device had three times more strokes than those who had a traditional open-heart procedure. They also had more complications with the arteries leading to their legs. Still, what other choice did I have? I thought being involved in something so revolutionary and challenging would be wonderful.

The operation was performed at the Scripps Green Hospital in San Diego, using the Edwards Trans-catheter Heart Valve

I passed all the qualifying tests for this experimental procedure, and went into the operation with the best possible attitude. But when I awoke in my hospital room, the doctor informed me they had to abort the operation because they encountered a blockage before they reached the valve.

"What does this mean?"

"We're going to try another way," they said. "You rest up and recover, and in a week, we'll try a different way to place the new valve."

Forgiving is the Attribute of the Strong

Sure enough, the Heart Team at Scripps-San Diego, led by Chief of Cardiology Dr. Paul Teirstein, called up Edwards Lifesciences, the manufacturers of the valve. The Scripps team was on the phone with Edwards partner doctors from all around the world, discussing the new procedure in minute detail for several hours. The proposed method called for making an incision directly under the rib cage to insert the new valve via a tube that would go through the bottom of the heart. Although the doctors at Scripps had never done it this way before, they were now confident it would work after consulting with the experienced doctors who had been successfully performing this procedure around the world.

As I lay in my hospital bed, recovering my strength to go through this second procedure, I feared most that everything I had worked so hard for all these years could come to an end if it didn't go well.

I thought about all the people I had met along the way who helped me. One of the things Betty and I have said for years was, "We didn't make a penny off the trial, but we sure made a million dollars worth of friendships." We never would have otherwise met all the people we met, or gone the places we went. It was all because of the trial, and even more, because we lost the trial! Had we won, we never would have gone to Japan. Think of it like, "If too much good occurs at the beginning, you fail to get all the bad that's necessary to make the good better!"

My fear welled up, but I felt such gratitude toward all those spending hours on the phone discussing how they could save my life. They valued life so highly they would do anything to save even the life of a ninety-year-old like me.

It reminded me of that expression, "Dying is easy; it's the living that's hard." That attitude is exactly what inspired me to participate in this experiment. If my being a "guinea pig" for this procedure resulted in its FDA-approval, if it could save other lives, it would all be worthwhile.

Suddenly I understood that expression "Forgiveness is the attribute of the strong." Many times I had heard "one of the most difficult things is to respond to cruelty with compassion, to forgive an unforgivable act," but now it all made sense. The men who beat me and killed my buddies had done the easiest, most animal thing. Their culture valued death over a life of shame, death over surrender. My former enemies deserved only my pity, nothing more. But dying is easy, and killing is easy. It's life that is hard. My doctors, so dedicated to preserving life at all cost, were the heroes deserving my attention now. They deserved my respect for advancing civilization forward one step at a time. That, I decided, is what our lives, however brief, are about.

Forgiveness is a Gift you Give to Yourself

I came through the operation with flying colors and felt stronger than I had in years. My recovery was almost immediate, and within a very short time, I was home and planning our long-awaited trip to Japan. Four months later, in September of 2010, I led our delegation to Japan at the invitation of their government. Six former POWs, accompanied by their wives or children, and the descendants of two deceased POWs received a formal apology by Foreign Minister Katsuya Okada.

Giving gifts is a very important part of Japanese culture, so I felt it was essential as part of our American Visitation program to have a meaningful gift for each of our POWs traveling to Japan to give to the people we were going to meet. I wanted this gift to not only express our friendship and how happy we were to be there, but also to tell our story and who we were. Thinking it over a long time, I finally decided a "Challenge Coin" would be the perfect solution.

No one is exactly sure, but rumor has it the "challenge coin" originated during World War I. The first one was a United States silver dollar used to identify a captured soldier as American when his fellow prisoner "challenged" the soldier for proof of who he was. I like to think of them also as a token of friendship, passed from one hand to another, privately acknowledging the challenge two soldiers shared. Our coin would be both a token of friendship, and a way to tell our story.

A good friend, Nic Wood, helped me design the individual coins for each of the four years we had the visitation program, beginning in 2010 to 2013. Each year's coin had a different design. Each year we made three hundred of them, with each POW receiving twenty-five coins to give to the Japanese people he met, keeping one for himself as a memory of this special occasion. The payment for manufacturing the coins was donated by another good friend for all four years.

The 2013 challenge coin, one of four different designs issued for each year of the visitation program, beginning in 2010.

Some of the POWs went to visit the camps where we had been imprisoned, and some to the mines where we worked. In addition, Betty and I went to pay our respects to Toru at his grave site. It was a very healing experience for everyone, and we all were very touched by the hospitality and graciousness of the Japanese people.

The Gift of Peace

Only now, looking back, do I realize forgiveness has been a work in progress; you don't ever separate yourself from it. We probably received this apology only because I already had forgiven, without even knowing it, rather than the other way around. Every fiber of my being had changed over a long period of time.

I choose to believe all things happen for a purpose, and that God has a larger plan. Maybe the answer to "Why me, God? Why me?" is "Why not me?" The answer to "Why did you take all my friends and keep me alive?" Maybe it was for my role in the healing between our two countries. Or maybe it's so I could be a little part of man's larger battle against hatred and tyranny, the fight for justice, honor and peace.

Now I realize forgiveness was not something I conferred on others after I decided they deserved it. No, it was something I deserved, a gift I gave myself: the gift of peace of mind. Through forgiveness, I moved from victim to survivor. Because of forgiveness, I am a prisoner no more.

Japanese Ambassador to the United States awards
Lester Tenney the Ambassador's Medal
for deepening mutual understanding and friendship
between Japan and the United States December 2, 2013

The Japanese Minister of Foreign Affairs,
Okata-san apologizes for his country's inhumane
treatment of American POWs during World War II

Epilogue

There is only one story left that should be told. It was when I finally learned, halfway through my life, that I didn't have to do everything all on my own, that it is no sin to ask for help. In my quest for a doctor's degree from the University of Southern California, I had to take the quantitative test for admission to the program. I took it, but I did poorly. I was allowed to retake the exam the following week, but without help, I was afraid I would fail again. I finally got up the courage to ask a friend who was an ace in math for help.

He was delighted to help, and asked me, "Did you know the test was 'open book?'"

"No," I said, "I didn't know that."

So with his coaching, I took the test again, and this time I passed it with flying colors, and was admitted as a candidate for the doctoral degree at USC.

What I learned from that experience was there is no shame in asking for help. It's a sign of courage, a strength I didn't know I had. Don't waste any more of your life thinking it's a sign of weakness. There is someone out there anxious to help, if only they are asked.

I tell you this because the end of my story is the beginning of yours, or of someone you know and love. This book is my "challenge coin" to you, my way of privately saying, "I know you have suffered. I have been there, too." It's also my way of challenging you to do the work that only you can do to restore yourself to the life you are entitled.

Tell your story. Train your mind to see what positives you've gained from your experiences. If you find you can't do these things on your own, be courageous enough to let others help. With all they know now about PTSD, there is much help available.

There is a branch of psychology called "Cognitive Behavioral Therapy" that helps train the mind to see the positive in all situations, and set attainable goals. Also, "Exposure Therapy" is available to gradually acclimate a person to their uncomfortable feelings caused by their "triggers." These skills that I intuitively used turn out to be among the most successful approaches in PTSD therapy today. The other is having the loving support of family and friends.

In fact, the turning point for me was love and friendship. The hardest challenge is to love and forgive yourself for the past, and to let go of the bitterness and hatred that has imprisoned you for so long. Let understanding and forgiveness free you from the prison of your mind. Let it allow you to use your God-given talents to take what has been deeply wrong, and find the courage to make it right. Then you, too, will find peace of mind.

That is my sincerest hope for you. May you find the peace you seek in the days ahead.

World War II Museum presents to Lester Tenney the Silver Medallion Medal for his unusual service to his country, 2013